WILL AI TAKE MY JOB?

Predictions About AI in Corporations, Small Business, and the Workplace

By: Matthew Rouse

First Edition v1.1
October 17th, 2023

MATTHEW ROUSE

Will AI Take My Job?
Copyright © 2023 by Matthew Rouse

All rights reserved. No part of this book may be reproduced in any form or by any electronic or mechanical means including information storage and retrieval systems, without permission in writing from the author. The only exception is by a reviewer, who may quote short excerpts in a review.

Cover by Matthew Rouse
Editing by Kari Rouse and Alicia Quin
Foreword by ChatGPT-4 (with human prompting and editing)

Printed in the United States of America and Canada
First Edition: October 2023

For Faith

(The concept of faith and my daughter, Faith.)

INTRODUCTION

2023 may become known in the future as the start of the "Age of AI." But is this the beginning of the end, or the start of a golden age of humanity?

And what does this mean for you? That's the big question.

Is AI going to "take" your job?

The short answer is, "it depends."

It depends what kind of work you do. It depends on how your work is regulated or how private the data is. It depends how much of your work is physically in-person and the environment where you do your job.

There are other factors like quality of connectivity, access to reliable power, security of facilities, access to hardware specific to AI systems, and many more.

The news telling you AI is going to "steal everyone's job" isn't helpful. It's way more complicated than that. One thing is for sure, AI is going to change the workplace and the world as we know it.

But just by picking up this book, you have significantly improved your chances of keeping your job, being more competitive in your business, or learning how to manage the "Age of AI."

This book is a combination of my personal experiences working hands-on with AI platforms, early access to developing tech, speaking with groups and audiences about AI and productivity, talks from AI conferences, and surveys on the topics we will cover.

You will walk away from reading this book with a vastly improved sense of the current state of AI, how companies and employees are approaching AI tools, how to best protect your future employment or business, and some wild predictions about the future that are sure to make you a hit at business gatherings.

I will let you know now that there will be some technical terminology scattered about in this book, but it is unavoidable in the discussion we need to have to determine if AI will take your job.

Let's get back to the task at hand: talking about AI.

Seemingly out of nowhere, generative AI exploded on the scene in late 2022, but only gained mass adoption in 2023.

It appeared in the wake of waning interest in Web3 and Cryptocurrency because of multi-billion dollar scandals and the lack of any day-to-day useful purpose in the eyes of the general population. But Web3 and blockchain is a discussion for another day.

Now, most information workers, students, artists, entrepreneurs, and marketers have heard of the most prominent AI systems: ChatGPT, Claude, Bard, Lambda, Jarvis, Stable Diffusion, Midjounrey, Eleven Labs, Dalle, Descript, and many others.

When it comes to the general population, the more educated people are, the more likely they are to have tried AI. Also, the younger people are or the higher their income, the more likely they are to have tried AI.

In a May 2023 Pew Research survey, roughly half of US residents have heard of ChatGPT but less than 15% have tried it.

For this book, I am taking for granted that you have a very basic knowledge of AI and have at least tried using an AI program. If you have not, take a few moments to give some free ones a shot.

Try ChatGPT or Bard, or download Pi on your smartphone and chat with it a bit. Maybe ask it to make you a recipe that includes three items in your fridge, to write a song in the style of your favorite musician, or ask to create an engaging presentation about your job.

Try an image generator. You can try using Midjourney or Dalle-2 to create an image. Make a unicorn in space or a group of dogs wearing business suits.

Maybe go to a site like Eleven Labs and type a sentence for an AI voice to read back to you.

You need to have an idea of what AI does and how good it is now. And remember. *This is the worst AI you will ever use.*

We will be talking about AI for productivity, how AI automation is threatening some industries, how AI Agents can handle entire projects, and AI Developers that can code applications.

We also need to have a discussion about AI ethics. What does it mean to "ethically train" an AI system? What data is public, protected, or private? What does copyright mean in a generative AI world?

And then, we're going to look forward to the future and talk about how embedding robotics and sensory devices with multi-modal AI systems is going to create Autonomous workers. The robots of science fiction that are being developed as I write this.

Also, no discussion about the future would be complete without talking about AGI (Artificial General Intelligence) and the possibility of creating a Superintelligence. What are the threats and benefits to humanity? How will AI companies, advocacy groups, and political groups make future systems safe, or "aligned" with the goals of humanity?

The future of AI is the collision of many technologies and discoveries. It's been said that in 2023, there was more advancement in AI than in the previous 20 years.

AI is seeing truly exponential growth.

"In a properly automated and educated world, then, machines may prove to be the true humanizing influence. It may be that machines will do the work that makes life possible and that human beings will do all the other things that make life pleasant and worthwhile "

- *Isaac Asimov, Robot Visions*

CHAPTER 1: THE CURRENT STATE OF AI IN THE WORKPLACE

The only thing we know for certain is that work, as we know it now, will change.

Any work involving data analysis, software development, digital design, customer support, writing and editing, marketing, acting, game design, project management, virtual assistants, borrowing and finance are about to change for good.

This is by no means an exhaustive list. There are countless other tasks and duties that could end up being automated which make up the majority of most people's workday.

This alone doesn't mean we will lose our jobs. In many cases, it could improve our job. Relieving us from the repetitive, tedious, or arduous tasks holding us back from doing our best work.

However, some people cannot see the forest from the trees. They lack the experience or technical knowledge to grasp the full potential, risks, and implications of AI by only concentrating on its current state.

Someone you know is going to tell you, "AI will never take my job!"

They refuse to believe it can happen, even if they work in one of the aforementioned industries. Besides, they are good at what they do, and a machine can't replace them, dammit!

They may be right.

But I would wager that they should take a long, deep dive into what's happening with AI before they strut their stuff so confidently.

Remember this: the current AI you are using is the worst AI you will ever use.

It only gets "better" from here. But "better" may not be the right word. I would say, "more capable," is a more accurate description.

Our brains are simply not designed to extrapolate the future in an exponential way. Because of this, it is easy for folks to misunderstand or simply be wilfully ignorant of what is to come.

To get some perspective on exponential growth in technology, we can look at video games consoles, which is something I know well having worked briefly in the video game industry. We will compare the Atari 2600 (1977) to the recent Sony Playstation, better known as the PS5 (2022).

Now, comparing an Atari 2600 to a PS5 is like comparing a bicycle to a rocket.

The PS5 does 235,294 more computations than the Atari 2600 every second.

The Atari wasn't even capable of creating a single polygon, which are the little 3D triangles used in modern video games and modern CGI for movies and television.

A PS5 can process roughly 10.28 Billion polygons... per second.

If you were to count every polygon created in a single second by a modern video processor, it would take you approximately 326 years.

Just think, in training an AI like ChatGPT-4, it takes thousands of more powerful graphics processors than the PS5 has and runs them 24 hours a day for months at a time.

Comparing the first GPT-1 (2018) to a current AI like GPT-4, Bard, or Claude-2 is also like comparing a bicycle to a rocketship. A more accurate comparison would be the mental capacity of a toddler to that of a young teenager. And it took a lot less time to make that leap than it did to go from an Atari to a PS5. It only took a few years.

The speed of computation is unimaginable.

Wrapping our primate brains around exponential technology is a difficult thing. We're not built to think that way.

An excellent demonstration of exponential growth is called, "The Rice & The Chessboard."

Imagine a simple chessboard (64 squares). You place a single grain of rice on the first square and double that on the second square, two pieces of rice.

Double it again for the third square, placing four grains and continue this process, doubling the number of grains for each subsequent square.

By the time you reach the end of the first row (8th square), you have 128 grains on that square. It might not seem like a lot at this point. But it would take a long time to count 128 grains of rice.

As with our Atari 2600 evolving into a PS5, the numbers become staggering.

By the 32nd square (only halfway through the board), you'll be counting over 4 billion grains of rice for that square alone. By the time you reached the final square, you would require more than 18 quintillion grains.

That is so much rice that the amount on your last chessboard square would be as big as a mountain. But not a mountain of rice, it would be a mountain of sand, with each grain of sand equalling all the rice that exists in the entire world.

The point I am making is that the "next AI" (referencing the next GPT or the newest version of an image, video, voice, or music creating system) will far surpass the capabilities of the last one.

In our case, the "next" one is likely less than a year away. And the one after that less than two years away.

ChatGPT-4 is twice as capable as ChatGPT-3.
ChatGPT-5 is four times as capable.
ChatGPT-6 will be 16 times as capable... and so on.

"This AI" – referring to all the current systems – is pretty good, but it isn't great. The next one will be great. And the one after that will be amazing, and the next absolutely astounding, as long as we don't hit some kind of unforeseen problem with scaling the technology.

The growth in power and capability and speed of these models will continue to improve. Is it for the better?

Author's Note: These are theoretically estimated in increased capability, but in testing, the models seem to be 5-10x as powerful as the previous models.

A recent benchmark test using more expansive testing found that ChatGPT-4 was 5x more capable than ChatGPT-3.5, and 10x ChatGPT-3. The models seem to scale by magnitude but we don't know if this will stay constant.

If scaling by magnitude stays consistent, then instead of GPT-6 being 16 times more capable than GPT3, it will be one thousand times more capable.

The scaling of this technology is why people are concerned about the future of these systems. How much more capable do they need to be to do what you do?

That's what we're going to talk about.

Why Your Friend Bob Doesn't Think AI Will Take His Job

Let's talk about the nay-sayers and non-believers who refuse to believe that AI will change anything.

They are dead wrong.

I have seen the future, so to speak, and the capabilities of AI are unquestionably going to change life as we know it. I feel very privileged to have been given access to unreleased versions of AI software, and I am involved in a number of alpha and beta tests of upcoming products.

And let me tell you, I have seen some things that made me curse under my breath in disbelief. They are what I like to refer to as, "indistinguishable from magic."

A reference to the Arthur C. Clark quote, "Any sufficiently advanced technology is indistinguishable from magic."

But the nay-sayers are everywhere, trying to protect what they have by yelling to the rooftops that AI is evil magic, but also that it has no functional purpose.

But it can't be both, Bob. Is it useless or is it going to take over the world? Make up your mind, Bob!

One of these nay-sayers attempted to publicly undermine my AI musings on a social media post. They commented, "If AI is so smart, why don't you just have AI plagiarize your entire book for you." *Yuck, yuck. Good one, smart guy!*

Let's put the plagiarism misconception aside, you probably <u>are</u> curious to know if this book was written by AI.

The answer is no. However, I used several AI programs in the process. I like to call it, "partnering with AI," as I wrote about in my previous book, PEERtainment.

Yes, I used an image generator to help with the cover art, and ChatGPT-4 to help with the layout, the chapter titles, rewording complex sentences, and to help me explain difficult concepts with more clarity.

An AI was not used to write the book itself.

This is for a number of reasons:

1. AI writing systems are good, but not THAT good, yet. I don't feel that they are up to the standards of writing required for an educated and attractive reader, such as yourself.
2. Ironically, AI isn't up to date on AI advancements. The current Large Language Models (LLMs) you may be familiar with (ChatGPT, Claude, Bard, Lambda, et al.) are only trained up to a specific date with information.
3. Right now, in the USA for example, works created by generative AI cannot be used for copyright because the work was not created by a person. That will be important later as a reason why AI may not take your job.

The second point is important, that AI systems aren't up to date on news and such.

An AI system is similar to a history book in this way. It was trained on information up to a certain date, and once the model is published, it doesn't know anything "newer" than what it was trained on.

(Author's note: An AI can be given additional information in real time but there are a number of security and safety reasons they aren't up to date on current events and research. We will talk more about this later in the book.)

That said, context can be provided to a system, or even training them with additional data or private company data, but we will talk more about that later.

Now if you really want to have a coherent argument with your nay-sayer friend, Bob, you need some technical details.

We're going to get a little bit technical here, but this understanding is vital to the rest of the book. It may just be your "Ah-ha!" moment.

Virtually every company on the planet was caught off guard by the release of ChatGPT, including many huge players in the Artificial Intelligence industry.

The technology behind the chat-interface for a "Generative Pre-trained Transformer" (hence ChatGPT) is revolutionary.

Never before have people been able to "chat" with an AI. Nor did anyone really think the general public, outside of data scientists and researchers, would ever want to do it.

- **Generative** because it generates language.
- **Pre-trained** because it was taught with hundreds of millions or even billions of pages of text and data.
- **Transformer** is the type of neural network used to build the AI model. I won't get into the software engineering side of it, but let's just say *it's complicated*.

The year 2023 marked a significant turning point in AI advancements, with more progress than the combined developments of the prior two decades.

This surge is now fueled by global investments amounting to hundreds of billions of dollars.

Additionally, the convergence of certain pivotal technologies has led to a rapid emergence of AI companies in the industry, including advances in vector processing - previously used in graphics cards for video games and 3d modeling, but very well suited to the structure of neural networks.

Why Do People Think a Chatbot Could Be Dangerous?

There is a rare interview on the Dwaresk Podcast with Dario Amodei, CEO of Anthropic, which I highly recommend listening to. It may be a bit too technical for people not familiar with software development, but there are still a lot of valuable insights in there.

What I inferred from this and other experts is that the initial problems with LLMs seemed insurmountable to most AI researchers. There didn't seem to be a good commercial use for a system that couldn't answer 2+2 correctly, like GPT-1.

Most companies working with LLMs had abandoned the GPT model or at least put it on the back burner. The research was interesting but not the kind of research that would lead to anything important or profitable, so most let it slide. No one figured it could possibly turn into anything dangerous.

The systems would get basic math problems wrong, and would hallucinate fiction when asked for facts. Without solutions to these problems, most large companies abandoned their research into these models in favor of other types of AI.

Dario Amodei, having worked on GPT models up to version 3, said that he realized early on that the more you scale the parameters and the data, the more the AI model will scale its capabilities. It was an educated guess and he and some folks at OpenAI agreed.

He was VP of Research with OpenAI before creating Anthropic, the maker of Claude-2, essentially a competitor of OpenAI. After working on the first few GPT models, he saw the power of them but wanted to take the company in a different direction. Where Sam Altman's OpenAI is focused on creating a Superintelligence or AGI (Artificial General Intelligence), Anthropic is trying to create a safety-first based AGI model by solving the problem of ensuring AI/AGI is in line with human values and ethics, however vague that may be at this time.

A Simplified Look at How AI Works

Parameters are essentially the variables an AI system uses to make predictions. The more parameters, the better the output.

Once you have the neural network set up, you need to train it. Instead of telling it exactly what to do, as you would with traditional software, a neural net is given examples with information about those examples. Then it is tested on its ability to identify additional training data.

As promised by the title of this section, here is a simplified example of training a neural net to create an AI.

You supply the system with 10,000 photos of a cat and label them all as cats. You feed the system another 1000 photos of cats and animals and objects that look somewhat similar to cats. You then test the AI to see if it can identify which photo in the test data is a cat or is not a cat.

When it correctly identifies the photo as a cat, the neural network will weigh the connections in its network that led to the correct decision. When it gets one wrong, you correct it and it will modify its neural net accordingly.

And then you do this with thousands, and then hundreds of thousands, and then millions of examples. There are several hundred or thousand rounds of training and testing done and tweaks are made to the system. More data is given to the system and so on.

The more initial accurate data the AI gets, the better it will be. The more total data the system can be given, the better "trained" the system is.

Got that so far?

1. The parameters are the bucket and the data is the water.
2. The bigger the bucket, the more data you give to the AI.
3. The more data you give to the AI, the better the output and the more different things it can accomplish.

At this point, most data scientists do not see a limit to the theoretical ability of these systems to scale. The biggest challenge coming up is the limit of hardware and electricity to power them, but that point is a long way away.

The ability to scale their capabilities is the reason that industry experts think they could become dangerous.

Dario joked about having to protect a powerful AI system of the future, and the setup would be, "a data center next to a fusion reactor beside a bunker."

The scaling of the system follows something we don't understand yet. There is no process yet to "X-ray" an AI model and see what it is doing or to reverse engineer why it is able to create what it creates. You may hear AI industry folks talk about *mechanistic interpretability*, which is the fancy name for this reverse engineering process.

99% of the people you hear talking about LLMs in the news media and on social media don't have it right. It is not a plagiarism machine reshuffling words around, technically they run on tokens - not even thinking in full words to begin with.

Author's Note: A Token is not even a word most of the time, but part of a word. It could be a symbol or a number, or even a single syllable. Roughly translated, a token is the equivalent of ¾ of a word.

A GPT is a prediction system designed to mimic how our brains work. By predicting the next token (or what word comes next) and then having weighted probabilities, it gets really good at delivering text in a coherent way.

But as more capabilities emerge, the idea of alignment is coming up more and more.

Alignment means, "Are the goals of the AI aligned with the goals of humanity" (or at least, the goals of the creator/owner)?

Because we can't see how it decided to predict a series of tokens which become the output it produces, we can't reverse engineer the system to see why it created the output.

We can't see how an LLM helped you script that movie about the wealthy New York attorney and the small town Canadian Lumberjack. In the same way that we can't figure out how your neighbor came up with the idea to paint their house orange with a gold roof.

Similar to the complexity of the human brain with its billions of neurons, AI systems like GPT operate with billions of parameters. These parameters help the model process vast amounts of data, including fragments of words, symbols, or numbers known as tokens.

Although we can study and probe these models, understanding the intricate workings of their billions of parameters, especially as they perform rapid and complex calculations, remains a daunting challenge.

And part of the potential misuse of AI is that it's just as happy to help you create a biological weapon as it is to cheerfully write a poem about cats riding unicorns. This is why companies use a process called "guardrails" which we will cover later in the book.

Data engineers don't exactly know why giving a neural net millions of tokens allows it to understand basic sentence structure, but giving it hundreds of millions allows it to understand how to do arithmetic and billions or trillions "should" allow them to understand the physics of the world in which we live.

They don't know why it can go from writing good sentences in a small model, to writing coherent instructions of complex processes in a larger AI model. There are a lot of theories, but to my knowledge, no one has cracked the code yet.

Currently, they understand that the system will keep learning more and will be more functional, the bigger you make it and the more data you provide.

If you ask Dario Amodei, CEO of Anthropic, one of the leading AI foundational model companies, how long before the new systems are at "human level" capability, he had this to say.

"In terms of someone looking at the model and even if you talk to it for an hour or so, it's basically like a generally well educated human, that could be not very far away at all. **I think that could happen in two or three years.**"

How Is AI Being Used In Industry Right Now?

There is a meme of a cartoon dog sitting drinking coffee at a table in a cafe that is on fire. He is saying, "This is fine."

This is how I would describe the scene at most corporations when it comes to AI systems.

- The board is asking what the company's AI plan is.
- The customers are asking if the company is using AI.
- Your staff could be using AI without your knowledge.
- Vendors could be producing work with AI without your knowledge.
- Staff could be creating things with AI such as images, videos, or products without an understanding of how copyright or intellectual property laws affect them.
- The CEO wants to know what AI is and how it can increase

productivity or reduce costs.

- Legal wants to know if we can even legally use AI or not.
- I.T. is worried about data security, improved phishing attacks, and exposing company assets to third parties.

The big problem is that no one knows if and what they are allowed to use and it's basically a free-for-all right now.

The next major problem is that no one in the organization has a good understanding of different types of AI. Few, if any, understand how they work, or what the risks and benefits are. Rumor and conjecture are the only information being spread about AI and this creates false narratives.

It is difficult to find staff with any AI training or experience, so how do you get actionable advice to create company policy and frameworks?

If those problems weren't enough, nearly everyone in organizations are worried about layoffs because of current economic changes or because of future natural disasters, and now they are also worried that AI could take their job.

Schools are back in session and I have only heard of two school systems so far in all of Canada and the USA that have a comprehensive policy on generative AI. Schools are trying to make policy around AI based on ChatGPT-3.5, when GPT-5 will likely be released before the end of the school year.

This is another common issue. As we mentioned before pertaining to some individuals, the same goes for organizations. They are making decisions based on the current AI, not the future AI. And as I demonstrated earlier, the capability of the next versions of AI will be exponentially improved compared to current models.

In the McKinsey 2023 State of AI survey, 35% of companies said that they expect to decrease their workforce in the next 3 years. 38% of companies said they plan to retrain more than 20% of their workforce.

I think that we can safely say that AI has turned things upside down in the workplace and will continue to do so.

We (collectively) will need to get up-to-speed on the capabilities of AI, as individuals and as organizations.

We need to remind ourselves that things are changing, even if we can't immediately see those changes around us. And once the changes are visible in our industry or workplace, those changes will seem sudden and sweeping.

How about an example?

A company in India released a support chatbot to 1% of customers as a test in March 2023. (The podcast I listened to about it did not mention their name.)

They found that wait times dropped from an average of about 5 minutes to a few seconds. The calls lasted less time. The customers received the support and information they needed faster. The survey responses received were more favorable than with their human staff.

How quickly will a company act when they see a service improvement combined with a cost savings? By the end of April, less than 45 days later, they had laid off 90% of their phone support staff except for the most expert and the most productive. The ones who answered the oddball questions, the things the AI was not able to fix, kept their jobs, as well as the ones who were able to use AI to be more productive than the rest.

Once an AI system is set up and running, it is a trivial IT task to scale the access to that system.

But in larger organizations or industries that require more creativity and thought, physically complex actions, or are more traditional, the pace of change will happen more slowly.

I watched a video the other day of a commercial apple orchard that had a fleet of drones which can determine which apples are ripe and pick them. Dropping them into automated machines carrying the apple boxes. It reduced their dependence on foreign farm workers and reduced waste while improving quality.

This means that even if your work involves physical labor, it still may be affected by AI combined with other automation or technologies.

Even if you work in an industry or organization that is slow to change, this massive societal change will likely put stress on the existing systems, leadership, and personnel in a way they are both unaccustomed to and unprepared for.

Key Takeaways From Chapter 1

The Evolution and Scale of AI: AI models, like GPT, have rapidly evolved in capabilities and scale, yet the intricate workings of their vast parameters remain elusive, with much about their learning processes still unknown.

AI's Societal Implications and Workplace Transformation: AI's integration in the corporate world varies, leading to both transformative successes and societal challenges, as industries grapple with its potential and consequences.

Concerns and Considerations Surrounding AI: Despite AI's potential, its decision-making remains mostly obscured, raising pressing concerns about alignment with human values and the potential for misuse.

CHAPTER 2: WILL AI TAKE YOUR JOB OR WILL SOMEONE USING AI TAKE YOUR JOB?

Surprising as it may be, there are hundreds of thousands of people who earn their living as "content creators." I even have been to the first two CEX shows, short for the Creator Economy Expo. (If you are a content creator, you need to go.)

In my previous book about content creation, called "PEERtainment", I spoke about aligning the goals of business marketing and content creation. For example, creators of podcasts, Reels, Tik Toks, or YouTube videos need to align their shows with the goals of the platforms used to distribute them to the audience.

This aligning of goals is how you get success with your content marketing efforts.

I said, **"You need to partner with AI."**

And that is still the case when it comes to keeping your job, business continuity, or managing your organization.

I've heard it said many times, and this is true in the short term.

AI isn't going to take your job, someone using AI will take your job.

This is true because if you run a company with 15 employees and train them to use AI, they become more productive. Now, the company can have 10 people using AI who can do the job of 15 people. The company no longer needs to employ 5 people of those 15 people.

If the company lays off the 5 people who aren't needed to produce the output, did AI take their job, or did the other people using AI take their job?

In the small business world, the same is true.

Imagine two identical businesses. The first business keeps doing business the way they have always done it. The business next door runs more efficiently and lowers their prices while improving their service because of AI adoption. The first business can't compete and closes down. Did AI take those jobs? Or did the people using AI take their jobs?

I spoke about this concept with Mike Kaput from the Marketing AI Institute in Cleveland, Ohio, and I have heard he and Paul Roetzer both talk about this on their Marketing AI podcast, which is brilliant.

Many companies can use AI to improve productivity and keep all their staff, gaining efficiency, improving market share, etc.

But some companies do not have a product or market where making more widgets fits the business model. In many of these companies, a 10% increase in productivity will mean a 10% drop in staffing.

Some companies making projections about gains from AI improvement in productivity talk about retraining staff for other roles, making up for areas in their company where they are having trouble hiring, or even opting to offer early retirement for some staff members.

These are just some of the ways companies are figuring out what AI means to their business.

(Author's note: Listen to the Marketing AI podcast, but also consider listening to my show, the Digital Marketing Masters Podcast, where we interview people and discuss AI in different industries.)

In the vast majority of jobs, there are tasks that can now be improved or automated using AI. Many repetitive tasks or tasks that used to be laborious, like analyzing large amounts of data or summarizing long documents, are the low hanging fruit of AI automation. We will talk more about this later, but just consider that there are workers who will be relieved of these tasks and can be more productive.

For example, in my marketing agency, we used to take long-form videos, transcribe them, cut them into shorter vertical videos for social media, caption those, and create articles and post from the transcripts. This was a time consuming task and took about 14 hours to complete for a single video. Using modern AI tools, this takes 2 hours, and half of that time is just waiting for the software to do its thing. We can work on something else for that hour.

This is a 92.86% decrease in staff time for the same output. And honestly, the end result is better and more accurate than when we were doing it manually. We can spend some extra time proofreading and checking the output, and less time manually resizing videos and typing captions. (I even used an AI to calculate that percentage at the start of this paragraph.)

This freed up our production time to be more creative and find better ways to improve results for our clients. To make better videos. To produce more thoughtful blog articles. Making social media that was more interesting. It gave us time to bring on additional customers with the same amount of staff and resources.

WILL AI TAKE MY JOB?

But not every company can just make more widgets or improve their services. There is a ceiling on the demand for their work or their products.

Let's imagine a large company has 1000 staff members in charge of creating their product or managing their service, and that company can see a 10% increase in productivity.

They only have a few realistic options:

1. They can generate 10% more output with the existing staff.
2. They can reduce headcount 10%, since employees are the greatest cost in most businesses.
3. They can have employees work 10% fewer hours, which could give them savings from things like paying overtime, or could reduce stress on staff, lower defect rates, improve quality of output, etc.

AI is being added to most of the productivity tools used by knowledge workers and office staff already.

It will soon be added to other industries and tools as well. Even organizations who try to discourage its use will likely have staff using it behind their backs. For example, when AI was added to grammarly, suddenly most browsers were now able to use generative AI in writing without needing to visit an AI website. This makes it virtually impossible to block those systems.

When a school, college, or university bans the use of AI tools and calls it "cheating", they aren't improving education, they are just encouraging some people to become better "cheaters." AI exists now. Fighting it is a losing battle. The companies who make AI assisted writing and studying tools will be targeting them at students and students are going to use them.

The ones who are effective in using AI to streamline their work, decrease laborious tasks, and improve the ability of their teams to

25

create better output, will have an added competitive advantage. An advantage that will grow with every passing day that their staff are learning to use these new tools and capabilities, leaving other organizations further and further behind.

Every business is different, and each will have to make a decision about what they will do with improvements in productivity by their AI-enhanced staff. But you can bet dollars to donuts that companies owned by private equity firms or cost-sensitive organizations will take any opportunity to lower headcount. In many companies staffing is the highest cost, and if a company is looking at their books with a red marker in hand, staff costs are going to get cut.

(Author's note: I realize that donuts now cost more than a dollar which makes that saying obsolete, but I still think most people understand its original usage.)

I think the moral here is that, in the short term, maybe the next 12-24 months, AI won't take very many jobs directly. But the productivity gains and cost savings by staff using AI will contribute to some job losses.

From large conglomerates down to the solo entrepreneur, there are tasks that can be improved, automated, or done more efficiently with an AI tool.

Right now, people using AI are the biggest immediate threat to taking your job.

Key Takeaways From Chapter 2

AI Enhancing Productivity: AI isn't taking jobs; it's the people using AI to streamline operations and improve efficiency who are reshaping the labor market. This tool not only optimizes work but also shifts the labor landscape, possibly leading to job reductions.

More AI Doesn't Always Equal Fewer Jobs: While AI can

facilitate a reduction in workforce by automating various tasks, it doesn't always lead to job losses; many firms use AI to enhance productivity while retaining their staff, illustrating the variable impacts of AI on different business spheres.

Inevitable AI Integration: The infiltration of AI into workplaces and educational settings is unstoppable, urging entities to leverage the power of AI tools to maintain a competitive edge, and heralding a shift toward an environment where AI integration is not just beneficial, but necessary.

CHAPTER 3: HOW IS AI DIFFERENT FROM OTHER TECHNOLOGY CHANGES?

Before the phonograph started to become widely available in the early 20th century, pianos and singing were one of the main forms of entertainment in homes.

The invention of the phonograph didn't immediately displace pianos. It took decades for widespread use of the technology to listen to music by professional musicians.

The largest increase in phonograph sales was in the "Roaring 20s" because flat records had been invented to replace cylinder recordings. Most music was available and jazz and swing clubs were helping to also drive adoption of the technology.

However, there are still pianos. Just because a technology comes along that changes our culture, it doesn't always mean the previous technology is completely replaced. There is always an adoption curve, and there are always laggards to cultural or technological changes of any kind.

This fact is often lost on the people working in or reporting about an industry, especially those on the "bleeding edge" of technological advancement.

WILL AI TAKE MY JOB?

If you look at the hype around blockchain and Web3 technologies, it didn't match the rate of adoption.

Companies spent billions on "Metaverse" and called it a technological revolution. But every time I went to visit any non-gaming Metaverse spaces, they were deserted.

Metaverse didn't have a "ChatGPT" moment. It never had an AOL Online moment where "everyone" was getting access to the Internet for the first time, not just hobbyists, scientists, and "nerds" like me. I prefer "geek," thank you very much. Metaverse has not had its Roaring 20s yet. And it may not.

But why?

Metaverse was cool and interesting and had hundreds of billions of dollars of investment capital pouring in. So why didn't it take off?

First off, it was complicated.

You needed specialized hardware, software, and there wasn't really any easy interface to just log in. Even with Metaverse spaces that were selling digital property and such, you needed to install software, figure out how to create and connect a cryptocurrency wallet, etc. I had trouble getting some of the programs to work and I have decades of technical experience.

The Metaverse only had niche use cases for solving problems. It wasn't immediately useful for most people. The lack of utility beyond gaming was a barrier to a wider adoption of the technology.

When ChatGPT appeared on the scene in late 2022, you could type, "write me a book report about Shoeless Joe Jackson," and your homework was done. It was just as magical as the best of the Metaverse, but it worked without any hardware or software. It didn't require training to make it function, and no motion sickness.

AI is accessible. It's easy to use. And the infrastructure for its implementation already exists for the vast majority of people and businesses.

Is This The Death of Retraining?

When phonograph production outpaced the construction of new pianos, the piano makers had layoffs. But it was relatively simple to retrain a piano maker to become a phonograph maker.

If you lost your job as a piano maker, you could walk across the street to the phonograph manufacturer and get a job. The piano salesperson could become a phonograph salesperson. The times changed and everyone just moved on.

When ridesharing came to a new city and claimed the jobs of many a taxi-driver, they just signed up to drive for Uber or Lyft, many independent taxi drivers even arriving to pick up their rideshare customers in their taxicabs.

When the word processor was invented, you needed fewer secretaries in the Secretary Pool to type documents. Many of the people in this job at the time were retrained to do other tasks, such as becoming administrative or executive assistants.

The list goes on. But what if automation or technology comes along that takes a job, without replacing them with a new job?

When GM closed several auto plants in Flint, Michigan, the story of the popular documentary, 'Roger & Me', almost all the jobs in the city were lost. Every shop and restaurant and all the other connected industries relied on those jobs to fund their businesses as well, it wasn't just factory workers who lost their jobs.

GM closed those plants and opened mostly automated factories with access to cheaper labor in Mexico. Though GM did retrain some staff and promote people to other positions, the majority were laid off and out of work. They were sent to the breadline without any other local industry to absorb the workforce.

The deindustrialization of the "rust belt" of the United States was due to automation, lower wages in other countries, improved shipping and supply chains, and ultimately, to improve the bottom line for shareholders. As Michael Moore said at the end of the film, "As we neared the end of the twentieth century, the rich were richer, the poor, poorer."

I feel that it is important to point out that many corporations do not take the lives of their lowest wage workers into account in decision making. The factory closures in Flint happened while GM was earning record profits.

My own research has shown that many large corporations have the mentality of, "decision by spreadsheet." If they can shave a few dollars off the bottom line, they will, regardless of the human cost.

Not all organizations, obviously, but when it comes to companies with thousands of employees, bureaucratization of organizations leads to a disconnect between leaders and the concern of the front-line workers.

Workers from Flint were told by the government to "just move on," and find work in other cities. Over time, most people did. But the point here is that a percentage of those jobs were lost for good. The new jobs created and the less expensive labor in Mexico created fewer jobs than were lost.

The difference between the phonograph builders and the auto workers is that when jobs are replaced by automation, those jobs go away and don't come back.

Deindustrialization over the last 40 years has shown us that when virtually all the low-wage jobs in an industry are replaced by automation, there is nowhere else for those workers to go to find a new job in the same field. They need to change industries or they will stay unemployed.

Technology has always displaced workers and some jobs just aren't needed anymore, as much as the workers in those jobs wish that was not the case.

Cassie Kozyrkov asked in her Keynote at MAIcon (The Marketing AI Conference), "What happened to the Knocker-Uppers?"

This is a reference to a job that used to exist but is no longer relevant to the world we live in now.

During the Industrial Revolution, the alarm clock hadn't been invented yet. If you wanted to get up in the morning, you paid a "Knocker Upper" to come around to your house with a large bamboo pole to tap on your bedroom window to wake you up for work. This type of job was considered "unskilled labor" at the time. The more current term is semi-skilled or low-wage labor.

Until the proliferation of alarm clocks in the 1940s and 1950s, this was a job. A job held by a lot of people. It's hard to believe that the first AI program ever written was only 20 years after the disappearance of Knocker-Uppers.

The Knocker-Upper could leave his or her position and find another job. Because labor was in demand, automation hadn't really got off the ground, and off-shoring hadn't been invented yet.

In the modern internet-mobile-computing age, there are still many low-wage jobs out there, but AI automation is threatening to replace a new contingent of workers: those of us who are considered "information workers."

That is, you work with data or communication, and virtually all of your work is digitized. As Seth Godin says on his podcast, Akimbo, "If your job is moving computer bits from one pile to another, computers are really good at that."

We can work anywhere with an internet connection. We have the ability to work while we travel. We can move, like I did, out of the city and get a little hobby farm in rural Nova Scotia, with 60 "backyard" chickens.

But there is a twist in this automation story.

With current technology, an AI can be trained with all the information an organization has on a topic. It can assess the needs of a task and work on it often without any additional training and with limited supervision.

It can communicate with a person using a text chat, voice, or video interface and relay the pertinent information or take direction on tasks.

An AI trained in this manner, that can take action on its own, is known as an autonomous AI-agent. We will just call it an AI Agent for short.

Once it's trained, it's replicable.

If you need a single AI-agent, or a thousand, there is no hiring process, no HR, no employer contribution for taxes, no sick days, no time off. If you need more "staff," you just make another copy.

The AI agent(s) will work, and as many of them as you need are available at a fraction of the cost of a human worker. Essentially, you are paying for the development and the "compute," meaning the cost of the processing power to run the agent. The commoditization makes it cheap.

How cheap?

I wrote an AI Agent for my own website. Every time I log in to the website, it comes up with a topic from a selection of ideas and concepts I gave it. Then it writes a short blog post and emails it to me for editing and approval.

Each time it does this, it costs me approximately $0.006. Less than a single penny. And it accomplishes the task in roughly 20 seconds. I even used the ChatGPT to help me write the code to connect to ChatGPT's programming interface. I can already do this now, with the worst AI you will ever use going forward. Think about that for a moment.

The more work the AI Agent does, the better it will get. Learning from its experiences, but also the experiences of all the AI Agents in the company simultaneously.

If the AI Agent is a third party product, trained by additional data from other copies of the AI agent in other situations, it can assimilate those improvements into its own training. Learning from thousands of models in thousands of companies.

New, more productive models, can be re-trained on the existing data, improving the capabilities of the AI Agent.

AI Agents will be prebuilt for every niche, job, or industry you can imagine. They will be commoditized, making them cheap and replicable.

According to an analysis on startup incubator, Y-Combinator, "Infrastructure and Data Platform layer will likely converge to a handful of players with relatively commoditized offerings."

When AI models and infrastructure are cheap and available, most organizations will have them. AI Agents and other AI programs and systems we haven't thought of yet will be built on top of those foundational models that are commoditized and inexpensive.

And yes, AI will create some new jobs, but not as many as it replaces. When new jobs are created by technology, it's often skilled-labor jobs which are created and in this case it may be a combination of high-skill, in-depth knowledge, tradespeople, and creatives who will find new jobs in the Age of AI.

Individuals who cannot learn skills needed in the new economy will likely be unemployed or underemployed for an extended period of time.

There will be no jobs in their field of expertise available because the human resource pool will be overflowing with candidates laid off from hundreds of companies.

As with the auto workers of Flint, Michigan, those jobs will be gone, and gone forever. Because many of us now work online or remote, many of our jobs can be replaced by AI Agents who also work online in the same channels we use to communicate and do our day-to-day tasks.

But never before has it been the white-collar jobs, or even middle and upper management jobs at stake. There is even a software company in SE Asia using an AI model as their CEO. "Business has never been better," they said.

When asked about when AI models will reach "human level", Dario Amodei, CEO of Anthropic, had this to say.

> It depends on the thresholds. In terms of someone looks at the model and even if you talk to it for an hour or so, it's basically like a generally well educated human, that could be not very far away at all. I think that could happen in two or three years.
>
> The main thing that would stop it would be if we hit certain safety thresholds and stuff like that. So if a company or the industry decides to slow down or we're able to get the government to institute restrictions that moderate the rate of progress for safety reasons, that would be the main reason it wouldn't happen. But if you just look at the logistical and economic ability to scale, we're not very far at all from that.
>
> Now that may not be the threshold where the models are existentially dangerous. In fact, I suspect it's not quite there yet. It may not be the threshold where the models can take over most AI research. It may not be the threshold where the models seriously change how the economy works.
>
> I think it gets a little murky after that and all of those thresholds may happen at various times after that. But in terms of the base technical capability of — it kind of sounds

*like a reasonably generally educated human across the board.
I think that could be quite close.*

There is no historical precedent for the automation of the middle class worker on this scale. There is also no historical precedent to look at what happens when this large section of the middle class workforce are unemployed.

Once remote or digital workers are laid off, there will be fewer and fewer places to absorb that workforce. Anyone anywhere can work in the available positions since they can work online, allowing for the most skilled or lowest cost workers to be available.

The best, the luckiest, and the cheapest will find work. The rest will be relegated to the unemployment line. They will have to switch careers, because commoditized AI Agents will have taken over the majority of the work in their industries.

And if we think back to our example about Flint, Michigan, when the majority of jobs are lost in a region, those people are not affected in isolation. The supporting industries, local hospitality, retail, non-profits, et al., all feel the ripples of that loss. If the scale of the job loss is significant and the new positions created are not plentiful enough to offset the losses, this could be a recipe to trigger a depression or worst case, an economic collapse.

This is all speculative, so don't build that bunker just yet.

Perhaps there will be some form of Universal Basic Income (UBI) in the future, allowing us to survive if we can't re-enter the workforce?

In the 2030s, maybe autonomous robots will take over most of the dangerous and laborious tasks beyond the digital.

People will be left to do as they wish without the toil and trouble of earning a living. We may all live in a "Star Trek TNG" style world, free of the shackles of monetary and personal gain. But those are questions for the end of the book where I will talk about the cutting edge of futurism and the SciFi-like technologies that will shape generations to come.

For now, let's focus on what may happen in the next half dozen years in different industries.

Key Takeaways From Chapter 3

AI advancements lead to efficient but disruptive automation: AI technology is evolving rapidly, introducing cost-efficient solutions but potentially displacing many jobs, including those in white-collar professions.

Potential for unprecedented unemployment rates: The swift rise of AI could result in historic levels of unemployment, particularly impacting the middle class as AI takes on roles traditionally filled by human labor.

Barriers to AI adoption still remain: Despite technological advancements, AI faces barriers to mass adoption, including complexity in many use cases and a limited immediate utility for some jobs. This suggests that careful, user-centric training will be crucial for successful integration into daily work life. Without integration into our jobs, our companies may become obsolete, like the deindustrialization of the United States.

CHAPTER 4: RETAIL, ECOMMERCE, AND CUSTOMER SERVICE

There are three types of AI systems that will affect retail, service, and support the most in the coming months:

1. AI Chat systems
2. The embedding of AI into existing products, like Microsoft Co-Pilot, for example.
3. AI Agents that can take action on their own.

These will affect businesses and jobs in general in the next couple of years, but will hit the support service and retail sectors sooner than most.

A report from Crunchbase showed that in Q3 of 2023, one fifth of all global venture capital investment was in AI. These systems will develop so rapidly they will seemingly appear out of thin air.

The low-hanging fruit of AI software is called a GPT-Wrapper. It is called this because it is software which, at its core, is using an existing AI model, such as OpenAI, Llama, or Anthropic and the software is "wrapped" around it without having to build their own core AI.

A GPT-Wrapper is also quick to build for the very same reason, because they don't have to make the AI that drives it.

It is a SaaS program (Software as a Service) or can be a feature

WILL AI TAKE MY JOB?

in an existing software program such as a writing assistant, spreadsheet formula helper, or product description creator.

Because these systems can be created quickly and cheaply, they get to market faster. You may even be using some of these already.

Anything that follows this process is going to be disrupted more quickly than other sectors, because of the ease of creating the AI program.

1. Understand communication or language.
2. Look up some information or take action.
3. Respond with the results.

GPT-Wrappers are quick to build and easy to implement for this type of process. To keep things simple, we'll just call them AIs from now on, but I wanted to make sure you understand the reason this type of software is suddenly everywhere.

Now that we understand why, let's talk about how Customer Service and Technical Support are going to change.

Customer Service and Technical Support

Customer Service was first disrupted by offshoring. California alone has reported losing more than 600,000 jobs to offshoring since 2005.

Cheap labor overseas and the Internet allowed the transfer of customer service and technical support calls to places like India or Eastern Bloc countries. It has been reported that as many as 37% of all companies in the USA have outsourced support or administrative jobs to offshoring.

It was then disrupted by modern chatbots. Companies have been using software to text-chat with customers and report information to them on demand, like their order details, finding support articles, reporting social media abuse, and a number of other interactions.

The same goes for phone systems that understand some basic commands by language, called Interactive Voice Response (IVR) systems. They work on a system of transcribing what you are saying and checking if they have a response for keywords in what you have said.

No matter the system, at least it was better to receive automated assistance than the dreaded on-hold message.

"All of our representatives are currently assisting other customers. Please stay on the line, and your call will be answered in the order it was received."

There are some types of interactions that can be better served by software, such as finding something on a schedule, tracking a package, or looking for a template out of thousands of options. Often software is an easy choice.

But when it comes to interactions that require non-programmable logic, the chatbots quickly become frustration-bots. I think we've all encountered the person trying to get around the IVR by yelling into their phone, "representative!"

With the invention of AI technologies like ChatGPT, combined with real-time voice transcription and a text-to-voice emulator, we suddenly have the ability for our customer service AI to understand and respond to customers as a well-trained employee would.

Instantly looking up something on a schedule or a previous order information is already faster with existing chatbots or IVRs. A customer service AI can perform even more tasks more efficiently than a person ever could.

Because the AI system can now work outside the limited number of pre-programmed responses from support systems of the past, it can go from answering a small percentage of inquiries, to the majority of inquiries.

Unlike a human, an AI support agent has instant access to all the customer's data, the entire company's knowledgebase, order information, product information and reviews, real-time data, product information, news, weather... Whatever the system needs to respond to the query.

What it does not have is the ability to deal with anomalies. The weird and squishy questions that involve things that don't really make logical sense. The things never before covered in past calls or the support tickets. Weirdness that doesn't conform to the models it has been trained on.

For this, they need a person. But not any person, they need a well-trained, motivated problem solver.

And if that person is you, then you will keep your customer service job.

Historically, customer service and support has been a "butts in seats" problem to the powers that be.

"How do we hire as few people as possible to answer as many inquiries as possible, at the lowest cost possible?"

To the corporate bean counter, customer support is a cost and costs are meant to be minimized or eliminated. They believe to maximize profit you must minimize cost at all costs and could care less if the customers are frustrated or annoyed.

As I mentioned before, bureaucratization has created a chasm between the decision maker and the customer. Customer service is not important when you never have to talk to the customer. It's also not that important when you never have to talk to the support workers.

The support workers are just cogs in the corporate machinery, and even if they are offshore workers, they are still a cost. And we know what the goal is with costs when corporate policy is concerned.

Especially in monopolized industries. If there is no choice (or there are only a few choices) for the consumer, then it is more likely for the customer service to be minimal. Their only choice to avoid poor customer service and long wait times is not having the product or service at all. In some cases, like dealing with the government, this process can be time consuming, unavoidable, and excruciating.

Then generative AI appears on the scene.

Now, a company can create an AI agent or lease an AI system specific to their industry from a vendor... A vendor they probably already have a relationship with. One who provides their existing IVR or website chat system.

It can answer inquiries faster and at a dramatically lower cost. A cost that decreases over time. After the initial investment to set it up, their existing IT staff or vendor can manage the system.

Like the example we talked about in Chapter 1, the Key Performance Indicators (KPIs) for call centers improved with the use of an AI system.

- The time to answer a call or chat was reduced from five minutes to seconds.
- A larger volume of inquiries were responded to, because fewer people got tired of waiting and hung up.
- Customer surveys showed an improvement in how happy customers were with the support they received.

If a corporation is shown that they can get better results at a lower cost, what do you think they will do?

After analyzing the AI system and testing it, they will train the system on their own data, and then start testing it in the wild. The AI system starts answering inquiries and helping customers.

As long as it works, there will be a nearly immediate reduction in

WILL AI TAKE MY JOB?

headcount, or at a minimum, a hiring freeze, depending on the call center contract they have, or the structure of their support staff.

The next step would be to reduce staff and with a reduction in staff comes a reduction in supervision, HR, and technical or desktop support. Depending on the size of the organization, this domino effect could reduce headcount in other areas outside the call centers.

The AI system is improved with data from answering calls and chats. The vendor or IT staff fix some bugs, etc. Because of this improved system, less support staff are needed.

The company is likely just keeping the best of the support staff, or in some cases where offshore call centers are the front line, and higher level support teams are more localized, eliminating the call centers altogether. Relying just on their in-house teams for advanced support that the AI currently can't handle.

This can and will have a ripple effect on the economy, felt first overseas. As call center staff is eliminated, so are the supervisor jobs, support, facilities management, and so on.

This cascade of job loss by itself won't have a major economic impact on an economy the size of India or Singapore, but combined with job loss in other industries, it could be serious. These countries have a high concentration of jobs like support, call center workers, VAs, and other work offshored from the west which could mean they feel it more than other countries.

The jobs created by AI, will likely be positions in the company's headquarters or main IT hub. AI jobs will likely be local to areas where data centers and company facilities are located.

Even though people can work remotely, the security around company data may require these positions to be localized. In a high-security data center, there are sign-in procedures, security badges, facial recognition, cameras, and other security measures in place.

If you work in a call center, customer service, technical support, or a related industry, there are things you can do.

The same goes for companies that provide support. You will want to know how your company and staff can use AI to improve their work. If you can leverage AI for productivity and train your staff to be more productive, you could handle more customers and everyone can keep their jobs.

In-Person Retail from Small Business to Big Box Stores

As we learned earlier, customer service and support is the low hanging fruit when it comes to AI automation. This alone will likely cause a reduction in headcount in the retail sector. But there are other uses for AI in all sizes of retail operations from the shop on the corner to a nationwide "big box" chain.

Helping consumers get the assistance they need after a purchase is one thing, but AI is increasingly being used in product recommendations.

The last time I spoke with a person working at a Home Depot, they were quite helpful and knew exactly what I was talking about. But the time before that, I had someone who stared at me blankly and flat out told me they had never even "lifted a screwdriver before."

Obviously, in a Home Improvement store, that isn't very helpful to the customer. But times are tough for hiring, people need work, and stores need staff.

But it won't take long before there will be a helpful computer screen with a smiling digital associate who will have all the knowledge of every product, every service, inventory on hand, ordering, shipping, and how to handle almost every home improvement project and problem the average person has come across.

There will still need to be people in the store, but fewer of them, and the people they do have working will, unfortunately, need to be the less knowledgeable but friendly (and lower paid) staff member I mentioned earlier.

The recommendations for products will come from the system, and the people are just there to help people access the system and products, load or unload things, and so forth.

The systems will also know us so that if we are shopping online they will be able to give us recommendations and advice.

eCommerce and Online Shopping

When you shop online, especially if you are a return shopper, you are leaving a lot of digital fingerprints, as well as your order history, search history, shipping locations, payment methods, and other information behind.

This can be used to customize your experience or to personalize it. But adding my name to the top of the search page isn't really a useful customization. Just like Amazon's recommendation engine works wonders if I shop for my daughter by recommending things that are age appropriate for gifts and back to school and such.

But it also has a problem. It's algorithmic, but not intelligent. There is a meme I saw once of a cross-eyed dragon pretending to be Amazon's recommendation engine and saying, "You bought a toilet seat last week, would you like to buy another toilet seat this week? Duhr!"

Joking aside, recommendation engines are about to get really smart, really fast. AI systems will have access to your order history and other information, and use that to help you find things you need... And may not need.

Imagine having a conversation with an AI representative about your partner's preferences in gifts and style and hobbies and having it recommend you gift ideas.

But then, in the future, showing you (or them) ads for other products they would enjoy. Things they would enjoy based on conversations you've had with it, and not just the average of what people in your demographics like, which is how they work now.

Personalization will be backed with intelligence and understanding. Maybe not the understanding of the world that we have as humans, at least not yet, but understanding that people have preferences and those are multi dimensional.

Maybe it knows that I like heavy metal music or that I like both RPG games, Pathfinder and Dungeons & Dragons, even though they are very similar.

It could understand that needlepoint isn't the same as knitting. Maybe it will even know that buying a single toilet seat is probably enough for a couple of years, unless we start a new bathroom remodel.

Systems will be able to contact us or we will be able to contact them to have a discussion about our problems and ask them what product we need, instead of trying to "google" the problem first and then go find the product or service we need to solve it.

This means that bringing people to a business website could be a problem for smaller shops and marketplaces. The problem-solving content isn't needed in a world where I can ask the Pi app on my phone how to solve the problem and it will tell me. No clicking on links or search engines required. That is, unless it's very new or very niche - something the search engines won't be trained on until they are actively pulling in real-time updates. The solutions could also be "gated", meaning they are behind a place customers need to log into, but this also won't last forever.

Take, for example, the coupon code apps. You may have one in the browser on your computer or on your phone and when you go to buy something, it searches for coupons for you. What a great feature!

But do you know where those coupons come from? Other people who are using them. For example, when someone has a problem with a product from a store and the store's customer service person (soon to be chatbot) says, "Use coupon cs20 to save 20% off your order," the coupon app is recording that. As well as all the details of the transaction.

Then you go to the same website, and even though you didn't have a customer service issue, the coupon app gives you a 20% off coupon. Hooray you! But now the retailer just lost 20% of their profit margin from a coupon you aren't supposed to know about.

But, hey, their loss, right? Except that those apps are also recording all of your online purchasing behavior, no matter what it is. Medical, personal, private... You name it.

If you are a retailer, make sure you are creating coupons for your customers when needed and that those have limits and expiry dates. Also, if you want people to use coupons from coupon apps to encourage purchases, just send out the coupons to your mailing list or put them on your website for a bit to seed the coupons into those programs.

Once AI is used to track orders, handle customer service, and create coupons, it will be able to personalize each coupon to each user. Rendering the coupon apps and plugins only effective for coupons the retailers want to give out, or to the unsuspecting small business owner who hasn't implemented any safety measures against them.

Generative AI will be used to create product descriptions, put products into photos and videos that never actually happened, create mockups, and generate explainer videos of how to use them.

I remember writing hundreds of product descriptions for a shoe store a couple of decades ago. Trying to come up with interesting things to say about shoes over and over. "Meet the girls for brunch with this modern spin on classic women's flats."

This is a job that will partially or in some cases, be completely automated. If you do this, I really suggest a proofreader or a copywriter, as with any AI generated text that will be seen by the public.

Data analysis is another use case for AI that will be widespread in a short time. At our agency, we are already looking at sales data and analytics data to get answers like, "What are the products people add to their cart the most often, but do not check out."

These are ways to get insights into data that used to only be accessible to companies with the revenue to afford data analysts. Also, large companies will be able to get the information they need with fewer data analysts.

AI systems will eventually be able to make decisions, by having all the data on hand and having been trained to maximize profit. They will be able to adjust the price of products based on the season, sales trends, advertising costs, availability, and other factors. They will be able to advertise products while controlling costs and creating videos and social media that encourage purchases based on past behavior.

Eventually. And that is the key word here. That could be 18 months from now, it could be 5 years from now. **How long it takes to roll the technology out is a mystery. But it will arrive eventually.**

Also, remember the example of ride-sharing reducing but not replacing taxi service? Just because a technology exists doesn't mean everyone will implement it. There may be a lot of use cases where it is just not a practical or profitable solution.

Sam Altman has said, and I am paraphrasing here, that the AGI (Artificial General Intelligence) he is imagining at OpenAI will be

able to:
- create a product
- find a factory to build it
- negotiate pricing
- set up payment and shipping
- create the website to sell it
- market, sell, and ship the product

This is a long way off. But eventually, we may be competing against products and websites built and managed by AI.

And how would we know? If you buy from Amazon, you don't talk to an "Amazon staffer" or Jeff Bezos when you buy that toilet seat you need. You just go there and buy it, and everything is automated after that point with a few manual steps in between by people you never meet, except maybe the delivery driver.

But if we look at the effects in the short term, there are some industries that will be negatively affected:

- Improved data analysis means less data analysts.
- Generative photos and videos means fewer photographers and designers will be required.
- It will take fewer staff to manage huge inventories online, those who enter descriptions, fix product inventories, etc.
- Fewer staff means less HR, and less middle management, as well as a reduction in SaaS product needs and virtual assistants who all reduce their staff as well.

But – and this is a big unknown – we don't know if these efficiencies will lead to revenue growth and require more staff.

For example, the more Amazon sells, the more staff they have hired, but not evenly. The last mile staff have grown, warehouse and delivery, while the support, human resources, and technical staff have seen layoffs. In January, Amazon laid off nearly 18,000 workers and paused its work on a corporate campus near Washington, DC.

Changes Are Already Happening

Like we have seen with Amazon, companies are making changes to who they are hiring and what positions they are hiring for. The layoffs from many large companies, especially tech companies, are in support, HR, administrative, and other areas where the skillsets may be augmented or replaced with smart automation and AI.

Without sitting in the boardrooms of these corporations, we won't really know anytime soon why specific layoffs are happening, but I think we can make an educated guess. The writing is on the wall, and these companies do not seem to be laying off workers in areas where AI is not good, like delivery drivers, in the case of Amazon.

Smaller retailers will be able to take advantage of data analysis and large scale writing, product descriptions, and inventory management systems without the associated staff and costs. This will likely help them earn more with their existing staff, and I doubt most of them would have a lot of layoffs, opting to repurpose staff to other areas of the business.

Small businesses will eventually reduce costs related to support, marketing, and marketing automation. For example, they may not need a stock photography subscription anymore if they can use generative AI. Or they may use an AI Agent instead of a virtual assistant to book sales calls and handle their inbox and meeting scheduling.

Support will be the first to be automated, followed by generative AI for writing and images, and then eventually replacing administrative virtual or in-house assistants with AI Agents.

In chapter 11, I will talk about ways to stay relevant in the Age of AI and the rapidly changing workplace. You can skip to your industry and then skip to the end if you're in a hurry, but I recommend you read the whole book.

It's short, and the more of it you read, the better your understanding of the near future will be.

Key Takeaways From Chapter 4

AI-Enhanced Personalization and Convenience: AI is on the trajectory to drastically enhance online shopping experiences, offering deep personalization based on a user's history and preferences. These advancements could see consumers having interactive AI conversations to find the ideal product or service, significantly elevating convenience and potentially increasing business revenues through smart, personalized recommendations.

Job Displacement and Changes in Workforce Structure: The automation of various tasks like data analysis, customer service, and content creation could lead to job displacements, altering the structure of the workforce substantially. However, it may also foster growth and create new opportunities, indicating a nuanced future landscape where the focus will likely be on skills that cannot be easily replicated by AI.

Data Privacy Concerns: As AI systems become increasingly integrated into e-commerce, leveraging vast amounts of personal data to personalize experiences, there arises a pronounced need for robust data security and privacy safeguards. Balancing the enhanced shopping experiences with privacy considerations will be a pivotal concern moving forward.

CHAPTER 5: AI AND THE VISUAL ARTS

One of the questions I get most often is a variation around AI and the arts. The questions usually take one of the following forms:

- "If a person types in a prompt to an AI, that's not really creating art, is it?"
- "If an AI is used to make something, who owns the copyright?"
- "If I use an AI to clone a person's voice, who owns the recording?"
- "Aren't AI systems just stealing other people's work and putting all the pieces together like a puzzle?"
- "AI can't make art, it's not a person, right?"

Can AI compose music, write novels, or create art? Is what they create actually art?

What does this means for artists, musicians, actors, and designers, and *gasp!* writers?

Well folks, get ready for the lawsuits to start flying because the legal action around training AIs on copyrighted material like books, art, and music is just the beginning.

There is no copyright law, in my non-attorney opinion, that covers the questions generative AI is bringing to the forefront. Each country will have to determine what their take on AI and copyright means.

For example, I have had several discussions now around the topic of AI-generated or AI-assisted music.

The Music Industry

With existing technology, you can fairly accurately clone the singing voice of any voice you can sample.

Songs are being created and shared that have dead singers singing songs written by their widowed band mates after their demise. Another recent trend is using the distinct voices of famous dead singers covering popular modern tunes.

When it comes to the use of voices in music, or speeches, videos, voice-overs, etc., parody under "fair use" is the go-to defense, but what about things that are not for comedy?

And if I were to recreate a song that is out of copyright, and use the cloned voice of a deceased musician, who owns the composition? Do I own it? Is it able to be covered under copyright at all? Do I have to pay the family of the singer, or do I pay the owners of the recordings I used to sample from?

And what about making music? Something like Stability Audio or Suno can be used to generate clips of music or songs of any genre from a text prompt.

If a person with some music editing skills can use that generated music and pair it with a cloned voice, is the end result music? Is it a musical composition that they own? (It sure sounds like music…)

In the "pop" music industry, using virtually nothing but digital recording, digital sound processing, digital effects, digital editing, and autotuning voices, can we really say that digitally generated music isn't music?

And that doesn't even consider algorithmically generated music, which isn't AI… But that is a consideration for another day.

These types of conundrums will be battled over by courts for years to come. I don't have the answers, and I am not an attorney.

Will it affect the music industry? Sure it will. Maybe not a lot at first, but it will eventually.

The first segment of the music industry to see a reduction in sales will be stock music.

The ability to generate endless "original" stock music with a text prompt, and to set the exact length of the composition will be hard to compete with. There is also the issue of stock music triggering sites like YouTube to look for "copyright violations" in the videos uploaded using stock music.

Because a video that is shot by a human is eligible for copyright under the existing laws, then adding generated music into that video won't affect your ownership or distribution rights.

Another problem facing the music industry will be electronic music in general. For example, EDM (Electronic Dance Music) can already be partially generated from loop sites like Splice who can use their AI to select from the available music loops, ensuring there are the correct BPM (beats per minute) and in the right key.

It won't be long before these types of AI systems are generating the entire song and being edited by text prompt. The democratization of electronic music to anyone who can type, will cause an even greater flood of electronic music than there is now.

And if you can generate and edit music with a text prompt, then a generative AI program will be able to write the prompt for the music AI system. By combining the systems, it will be able to create the song, analyze it, edit it, and produce it.

Singing AI voices are getting better all the time and they are not far off from being mainstream-ready. In this case, the AI could write the lyrics and produce the singing as well.

WILL AI TAKE MY JOB?

And if we extrapolate these technologies out a few more generations then we see the real threat to the music industry. And that is generative AI music networks.

There will be nothing to stop the owners of "the airwaves" to produce their own musical content. For example, iTunes or Spotify could use an AI system that generates music according to your tastes.

It could analyze if listeners enjoy the music and if there are parts of the songs where people "skip" to the next song. Then it could rewrite the music on the fly and test it with other users. It could also create 100 or 1000 variations of a song, test it on the listeners and use their feedback to find the version people like the most.

Many musicians I speak to do not believe an AI can create original music. And I think that is partially true, but partially false.

A recent research paper used an AI called a Generative Adversarial Network to create photorealistic images of pets that don't exist. But not just cats or dogs that don't exist, but making animals that are completely fictional.

A Generative Adversarial Network (GAN) is a type of AI system where one part tries to create something, like images, and another part tries to tell if it's real or fake, helping the first part get better at making realistic things. This same technology can be used to find things which are not in the training data. For example, creating a pet that has the attributes of a pet, but no set of characteristics matching any other pets.

This means we can train an AI system on music - all available music. Then we can use a GAN to have it generate music that sounds like a certain genre or type of music but does not conform to any music it has been trained on. This means it will make an original piece of music. It's not really creative experimentation or the touch of the Muse in your dreams… but the end result is still original music.

55

As with most of the arts, there is a recorded or printed version and a live version available to most flavors of art.

You can play live or record. You can paint and then make prints. You can produce a live play, or a movie. You could carve a masterpiece and then photograph or video it.

And this may be the way to ensure that AI does not take your job in the arts. I firmly believe that the pendulum always swings both ways, for all things. Call it a realist version of the yin and yang.

As AI becomes more prevalent in every facet of our lives, the will to grab onto something "real" will become much stronger. The more everything we see and hear is generated digitally, the more people will gravitate toward human experiences.

A lot of people are happy to "take what they are given" when it comes to the media. But there are many people who will want something more. These are your people.

The ones who want to know you and your story. The people who care about how something is made versus just the end result.

These folks will grow in numbers and interest. Wanting live music at events, concerts, and music festivals, which will start to push "real" and "human" in their marketing. Live shows and events will grow in popularity. Not back to what they were pre-internet, but it will increase from where it is now.

Painting, Photography, Design, and Illustration

Generative AI is already disrupting the design industries. At MAIcon, the marketing AI convention in Cleveland, Ohio, I spoke with two designers who said they had lost some of their clients to AI and that was back in July of 2023.

I ran a small poll on LinkedIn one time where people had to guess which Maud Lewis painting was AI generated. Most of the people guessed for two of the four paintings shown. The trick was, all of them were generated. (Maud Lewis is a famous Canadian Folk Artist who lived in rural Nova Scotia.)

Like with the invention of Canva, which brought the power of vector art to those untrained in advanced tools like Adobe Illustrator, designers started to lose some of their grip on the business world. Especially in the small business and non-profit sectors, you no longer needed an arts degree to make an advertisement or social media post that looked professional. (Or could pass as professional to the untrained eye.)

For the most part, digital design software has constantly been moving the goal posts for digital artists and illustrators. With the tasks of replacing font design going away, then clip art, then layout, print setting, and now full designs are easy to make and edit from templates.

It was not that long ago you couldn't print something at home. I remember selling some of the first color home-office printers in the 90s when I worked at an electronics store called Future Shop. In 30 years, the majority of the tasks in the printing and design world have been moved into the hands of the untrained.

For better or worse, digital design and art has been democratized and commoditized.

From the eye of the artist, digital design has gotten worse, and I agree. You don't have to look very far to find a terrible design that should have been made by a professional.

From the perspective of a business owner who now pays pennies on the dollar to get advertisements made, social media posts created, or is making their own print materials, it's both a cost and time saving.

Companies with "unlimited" design like Design Pickle or hiring out of country VAs to do design tasks have even made getting semi-professional work easy and cheap.

And we all know that there are three options when it comes to work. You can only choose two of the three:

1. Good
2. Fast
3. Cheap

But generative AI, and AI-assisted design tools can now give us all three at once.

Look at the integration of AI in Adobe Firefly, Photoshop, Canva, Microsoft Designer, and even right in the Bing Browser. You will soon find that for the vast majority of people's needs, no designer or illustrator is required.

Sure, there are cases where you want something "the AI" just can't make, or can't easily make, and those use cases will become fewer as new generations of tools become available.

For the photographer, as with stock music, stock photography is also one of the first to get hit. Generative AI is being used to create similar photos to stock, but where no royalties are required. And when it comes to the copyright and ownership angles, you don't own the stock photos unless you are the photographer. So that isn't a consideration for using generated versus stock either.

Our marketing agency has been threatened with legal action over stock photos several times, and we are quite careful about the licenses for photography. We ensure that we are using things that we are allowed to use. This doesn't stop the legal harassment, something that doesn't happen with generated photos.

In one case, someone who worked with our agency had modified a photo from a news article as an April Fools Day joke. We were threatened to pay more than $12,000 (USD) for the use of the image (6 years after the fact).

By explaining what was happening to ChatGPT-4, it was able to create a legal letter for us in defense of our fair use, and the opposing attorney agreed and dropped the matter. (Another use of AI, though we did consult with an attorney, and you should too when it comes to any legal matter.)

Liability and ownership are also issues. I understand that photographers need to be paid for their work and their skills are invaluable. We hire photographers and videographers often. But I can also understand, as a business owner, that ownership, rights, and liability are considerations.

A use case often overlooked about AI is generating similar photos. For example, you can find a stock photo of what you are looking for and upload it to a generative AI tool and ask it to make a similar photo. I know this is crossing a currently unresolved legal line, but I am telling you it is possible. And not just possible, but it happens every day.

I have also heard from photographers that generated photos aren't high quality. But there are tools called "up-scalers" that can increase the DPI (dots per inch) of any photo. Image AI programs can recolor old photos, reduce blurriness, replace missing sections... And the quality of photos from a program like Midjourney have improved by 10x in the last year alone.

There is an AI tool in development right now that does "object placement in 3-dimensional space using AI." (It was unnamed at the time of writing.) The idea is that you can talk to it and upload your photos, telling it to "place this teddy bear on the kitchen counter."

You can take a stock photo or any photo and then take a photo of your product and place it into the photo. The tool will figure out the size of the product, the size of the photo area and correct for light and shadows.

There is also the way stock photography is tracked. If I were to drop a stock photo into an AI editor and use generative AI to replace sections of it, or add more around the photo, such as a generative zoom out, the finished photo would be undetectable by current methods to find it has been used. And if they buy the license and edit it, is that ok?

Even with illustration, comic art, sketching, etc., image generators can create these works. They can even be told to create them in a certain style or in the style of a certain artist if the system was trained on that artist's work. The legality and ethics of training the systems on artists' work is too large a topic to discuss here, but as the tools exist now, you can do this with them.

If you use an AI like Stability, Dalle, or Midjourney, you can prompt it to generate cartoons and illustrations for you.

"Pencil sketch of retired men sitting at the bar top, in the style of political cartoons, white background" will give you a cartoon sketch. Drop that into Canva and add the text and you've got a pretty convincing cartoon.

You can take a selfie of yourself and upload it and tell it, "superhero in the style of comic book art," and turn yourself into a comic book superhero.

Videographers, Actors, Film, and TV

For videographers and actors alike, AI is changing the entire sector of video, TV, and cinema.

CGI (Computer Generated Imagery) has been used in film for decades now, all the way back to the movie Tron (1982). This film was made with more than 20 minutes of digital animation, something that had never been done in a feature film at the time.

On a personal note, I remember seeing Tron in the movie theater when I was just 10 years old and as an 8-bit computer nerd at the time. I scarfed down popcorn while in awe at the sound and the visuals, meager by today's standards. The "AI" in the movie, known as the Master Control Program, has stayed with me since. It could think and it could act on its own, though it was played by actor David Warner at the time.

AI is being used to create new advancements in the creation of video. For example, text-to-video creates short scenes without the use of actors, set designers, extras, writers, gap, casting, craft services, sound stages... And though in its infancy, this will be a big deal in the future. However, not immediately.

The two biggest current advancements that will have an effect on jobs for videographers and video industry folks are character replacement and digital avatars.

There is a program available to anyone with a credit card that is called Wonder Studio, and it does something I call "Character Replacement."

You can upload any video footage and click on a person in the video and replace it with a predefined 3D model, or one you make yourself.

As far as I know, and I am not an IP attorney, there is no law against licensing a stock video and then modifying the existing characters in the video.

I have already seen a short film created by a special effects house using Wonder Studio to replace actors used in the film with CGI aliens.

If you look at comic book movies as an example, people go to see the latest "Spiderman" movie, not to see the latest movie by an A-list actor. This is by design. If a movie studio can replace an expensive famous actor with any actor - and then replace them with CGI, the cost goes down. They own the IP, so they can still charge top dollar. Profit for them, and no big name actors needed.

Then there is also the idea of consistent avatars. If you were to generate a photo of a person (or use yourself), this likeness is called a digital avatar.

You can train an AI system to make more images of that digital avatar. Posing in different positions, clothing (or lack of), locations, etc. Using deep fake technology, you can combine stock, generated, or any video with your avatar.

You could train a voice AI system with your voice or create a new one. Programs like PlayHT or ElevenLabs can be trained to mimic your voice or you can create a new one using some sliders and controls like you would customize a character in a video game.

I probably don't have to tell you what this is going to do to the voiceover industry. The technology is already affecting the freelancer voice-over professional. Instead of hiring voice-over actors from Fiverr or Upwork, many businesses are opting to use an AI generated voice. And they are already very close to being indistinguishable from the "real" human voice.

A program like Descript for podcast editing can already learn from the voices it has transcribed and make corrections in the voice of the person speaking. In a creepy twist, it can also edit the eyeballs of the speakers in the video to make them consistently look at the camera. Not sure why we needed that, but it exists.

Now you have a voice and a video for your digital avatar. We can use lip-matching software to make the avatar speak in the video. This isn't science fiction, this is all possible with existing software and a little know-how.

Look at the rise of digital influencers and you will soon find many an "instagram model" or "tik tok influencer" who is not a real person at all. Just a digital avatar created to get likes and views... A process to try to earn advertising revenue or sponsorships. All without a "real" model.

But this doesn't have to just be used for social media. With a little help from digital animation and art tools, and some AI for upscaling, we will be using these tools to create TV and movies in no time.

In my estimation, the first independently made TV production movie or TV show made entirely by a single person augmented by AI will be out by the end of 2024.

This same technology will be used to spread misinformation, affect political campaigns, demonize or glorify individuals.

What To Do About It?

With illustrators, designers, and photographers, the key to longevity in your job is the ability to create "exactly" what someone is looking for.

This is the downfall of existing AI image generators. No matter how well you describe what you want, the image generator isn't going to get it exactly right. It's always going to be a variation on the theme you give it.

This gives the artist an edge. You can create to exact specifications, where the image generators can't. (yet). They will eventually be able to, but that is probably a decade out.

Try to determine ways to do what you do live. As the pendulum swings back from the "fake" or generated, to what is "real," many people will want more in-person experiences.

Some companies will want to promote their business or products by using marketing and other communications touted as "real" or "human." Just like there is "certified organic" there will likely be some kind of organization that touts, "certified human made" as the selling feature.

Focus on the things AI systems are not good at. Cultivate your relationships with companies who want or need the specific versus the general. You want to work with a company who wants an illustration or photo of an exact thing, not "photo of a girl catching butterflies in a field of sunflowers," because that photo can be generated by AI.

Key Takeaways From Chapter 5

A complex relationship between AI and the arts: There are impending legal battles over copyright issues. AI's potential to disrupt the music industry by creating "original" content is unknown to most people in the industry. There is the potential for a resurgence in the appreciation for human-made art as a counterbalance to the rise of AI-generated creations.

Movie, TV, and Film Industries: The rapid advancements in AI technology are reshaping the movie, TV, and film industry, introducing tools like digital avatars and character replacement, which democratize content creation but also pose ethical dilemmas, including potential misuse and the devaluation of human artistry. To maintain relevance, professionals should focus on the irreplaceable value of authentic, "human-made" content, leveraging their unique ability to meet precise specifications and offer real experiences. Balancing AI innovation with human creativity will be key to navigating the future landscape of the industry.

Generative AI is reshaping the Visual Arts in all sectors: By allowing for quick, affordable content creation, Generative AI is replacing some jobs and tasks in the visual arts, but raising ethical and legal concerns around copyright and ownership. The rapid advancement in AI tools is democratizing digital art and video, potentially compromising quality and originality, while fostering new opportunities for creativity and efficiency.

CHAPTER 6: HEALTHCARE, MEDICINE, JANITORIAL, AND CARE WORKERS

My daughter needed some new school supplies that we were unable to secure locally in the tiny rural town I live in, so we drove to the vast metropolis of Digby, Nova Scotia (population 7270) to visit a big box store.

While we were there, someone was moving a large blue floor cleaning machine down the aisle, and I gestured for my daughter to step out of the way. But it had already stopped.

That's when she asked me, "Daddy, is that a robot?"

And it was.

There was no person pushing the floor cleaning machine. It was a robot, or more specifically, a Service Robot.

The ISO defines Service Robots as ones which perform useful tasks for humans or equipment, but excluding industrial automation applications.

This floor cleaning machine isn't really an AI, it is pre-programmed with a route to follow to clean the floor, but upgrading this machine with AI would be a trivial task from a software engineering stand.

With the addition of a camera and microphone, and perhaps a speaker, the floor cleaner can become part of the staff. Keeping an eye out for safety hazards, helping direct those needing some assistance, or monitoring for things like fire or theft.

And just as they are used in big box stores, they are starting to be used in hospitals and other places where you want to keep the floors clean, but for a lot less than the cost of having a human being pushing a broom around.

I recently watched a demo of a bathroom cleaning "janitorial bot" used in office buildings but in testing for other purposes. It cleans and sanitizes restrooms but can't really "deep clean" right now. If there is a real mess, the robot would have to call a person.

The bathroom cleaning robot costs less to lease and operate than the average salary of a janitorial worker in the USA per year. Half the cost. And it doesn't need a vacation. (Or does it? We'll talk about the future and sentient AGI later in the book.)

AI For Medical Systems

A surgery assistant robot is another type of Service Robot. And surgery assisting robots have been around for a while now. As they are paired with smart AI systems, specifically trained on the videos of past surgeries, medical journals, and other surgery techniques they will stop being assistants, and start being surgeons.

A surgeon in a remote location can monitor several surgeries at a time and be on hand to "take the wheel" like you would in a self-driving car if there is danger. Harvard found that patients who had robot surgeries had fewer complications, shorter post-op stays, and lower pain scores.

WILL AI TAKE MY JOB?

Machine Learning systems now are used to read medical scans and reports, and in an MIT study, they performed better and faster than radiologists at looking for tumors or abnormalities.

Hospital management systems are being designed using AI to help navigate the massive amounts of data and ensure patients are being seen as efficiently as possible, with medical outcomes in mind.

We covered customer service in chapter 4, and how AI chatbots will affect jobs in support. There are a lot of layers of support in the medical industry from phone and chat support to front desk staff, internal support, technical support and helpdesk, the list goes on.

In Oregon, at a newly built hospital, there were large screens to welcome patients alongside the human-staffed desk. The touch screens allowed me to find services and checkin for some basic appointments, but once AI-driven, these screens could be a digital avatar.

A technology similar to what is already available from HeyGen could produce talking avatars, customized to our needs. A head-and-shoulders advocate to help you navigate an often complicated medical system.

You could show your healthcare card combined with facial recognition and it could generate the avatar for you, in your language and even in your preferred accent. It could even be designed to look a bit like you, to help improve empathy based on the experiences it has had with thousands of other patients.

Your medical avatar could help direct you to appointments, schedule or reschedule services, order your lunch from the cafe, or send your prescription to the pharmacy. It could even be a consistent avatar - sending you messages or taking your calls, so that you are dealing with a familiar face. A familiar face that was digitally created, but familiar all the same.

In the medical systems of countries which are socialized, any cost savings means the ability to improve care or hire more staff in another capacity.

Though we don't want to see people lose their jobs at all, the tradeoff in a lot of medical systems may be laying off phone center workers or customer support staff to hire more nurses and doctors. This would lead to better health outcomes.

In my research, it appears that most healthcare systems around the world are already overwhelmed. A combination of increasing costs, reductions in funding, and attempting to care for our aging population. A population which will live healthier and longer because of AI advancements in medicine and medical research.

I feel that most medical systems will take the efficiencies from AI in communication, support, treatment, and care without eliminating a lot of workers. Employees are difficult to find and train, and it doesn't make good economic sense to lay off people while you can't find enough skilled workers.

If you only have 50 people working in patient services and you need 200 to do the job effectively, you don't just cut those 50 people when you come up with a more efficient system.

You just do a better job, with the resources and staff you have available.

For displaced workers, they can be retrained for other needs in patient care, and also the medical system has an aging workforce, so early retirement may be another option in these organizations.

The World Economic Forum expects a 12.9 million person deficit in skilled workers in the medical field by 2035. They also estimate $750B is wasted annually.

If we can use AI to improve patient outcomes and reduce wait times, those efficiencies can mean that we require fewer high-skilled medical personnel such as Nurses or Surgeons.

When we use AI to reduce repetitive tasks, laborious work, some of the patient communication, support, rescheduling, reading medical charts and test results to assist in diagnosis, robot-assisted surgeries... These are all tasks AI systems are good at, or will be good at soon.

The people displaced by the use of AI for these tasks can be used to expand care, improve patient outcomes, reduce burnout, and to fill the shortage of skilled workers needed in medical systems worldwide.

Medical Research And AI

Medical research isn't all about discovering new drugs. But that's one of the use cases for medical research. AI is great at noticing patterns (or what is missing) from enormous data sets with millions of variables.

Advancements in AI are now being used in computational biology and chemistry, which are focused on discovering molecules useful in complex biological systems - like you and me!

Bringing a new drug to market can cost upwards of $2B and take 15 years. With the help of AI for discovery, analysis, and testing, that process could be an order of magnitude less expensive and time consuming. Drugs could be discovered, tested, and brought to trials in a year or two and cost millions instead of billions.

Machine Learning (a subset of AI) has been used in medical research for more than two decades now, but the way modern AI functions is different.

For example, in a recent live-stream from electric car maker, Tesla, they demonstrated a vehicle trained on thousands of hours of video and the beta versions they call FSD (Full Self-Driving). Though some said parts of it were simulated, but at the time of writing, I could not confirm or deny this.

This FSD was not programmed to look at all the data and then told what to do in each instance that matches the data. This is an example of programming. The code would tell the car that "a red hexagonal sign means stop."

But with a modern AI system, called a Multi-Modal LLM, the system learns from the dataset it is given, in this case video, audio, and text. (This is the multi-modal part - more than a single mode of training was used.) Similar to learning by example in humans, the AI is learning from watching and listening to what is happening when other people drive.

What this means for medical research is that you give the AI system all the data that exists about the biological process you are working with. Tests, scans, research papers, patient interviews, examinations, medical records, drug research, what worked or didn't in the past drug trials... And then you have it help you determine which direction to take the research.

What are we missing from the data provided? Is there an approach that would only be apparent from knowing ALL the information, more information than a single human could possibly consider at once.

There is also the advantage of using AI systems that can be trained on historical and real time data. A system like this could help with everything from running drug trials to looking for efficiencies in processes to manage care better.

An AI that is aware of the news, weather, traffic, and other factors can help provide appropriate staffing levels, prepare for potential emergencies, or notify staff of looming danger.

They could even send predictive warnings to patients who may be at risk from things like wildfire smoke or smog warnings with the steps to protect themselves.

The AI knows who has asthma... But, there would need to be

changes to medical privacy laws, such as HIPAA in the USA, but that is beyond the scope of this book.

Patient Care and Communications

From robotic pets to artificial companions on phones and tablets, the ability for AI to comfort people is well documented. In the absence of real people during COVID lockdowns, seniors in assisted living and memory care were shown to have improvements in quality-of-life when having these non-human companions.

Many small studies have been done showing improvements in patient outcomes when the written communication from their physicians was run through an AI system to make it more empathetic in tone.

Another interesting development in AI is the ability to give care without bias. Though there are instances of bias built into systems based on training data, this is different from having an unbiased look at data itself. The systems don't "believe" anything from a personal standpoint, so they have no motivation to treat patient A differently than patient B.

The systems, when used to analyze data objectively, will believe what a patient tells them. Sometimes people in marginalized communities have a hard time finding unbiased care providers so this could help level the playing field of diagnosis and treatment.

It is not impossible that there will be biases discovered in systems based on historical data containing these biases, but that doesn't mean the system is biased. It means the training data needs to be corrected - which is possible. In the future, another AI can be used to verify bias or negative sentiment is not present in training data for systems used with medical patients.

Whether the use of AI will translate to digital avatars of physicians or caregivers remains to be seen. However, comfort robots, sometimes called artificial companions, are already being tested with senior care and in medical facilities.

Autonomous robot companions may soon be coming to a senior or person with a disability challenge near you. With a multi-modal AI system connected to their "eyes and ears," these robots would be able to help with stable walking, getting in and out of chairs, monitoring prescriptions, light cooking and cleaning, and even calling medical personnel if there is a potential problem or emergency.

Home care workers are already understaffed in most post industrial countries. It is often a difficult, poorly paid, stressful job, and the turnover is high in these jobs because of these things.

Care robots could help bridge the gap for care personnel without dramatically reducing staffing in the short term. Long term, it is likely that care robots will take over a lot of these tasks, but that is more than a decade away at this point.

When it comes to counselling, suicide prevention lines, workers for domestic violences survivors and other mental health fields, chatbots and digital avatars are already being used by people who cannot afford help, do not know where to get help, or want to keep their use of assistance secret.

Another issue with these services is that Internet connectivity is not evenly distributed. People in rural or remote areas often have limited connectivity and cannot always have access to AI services.

There is also another layer of support services for caregivers and medical personnel, people who often have high stress levels and are often affected by burnout. AI can help to "counsel the counselors," but also can assist in helping to empower the organizations who support the people in these industries.

Organizations like RAFT who support the folks that work with survivors of domestic violence who are prone to "compassion burnout", which reduces their effectiveness and the time they can sustainably work in their fields. The organization is already using AI to assist in getting their message out to more counselors and medical staff.

I am not suggesting that you should use an AI to replace a trained medical health professional. I am not a doctor and this is not medical advice. And I'm not just saying that because my lawyer told me to. However, if you do not have access to professional help or do not know if you are ready for professional mental health services, it is an option that is becoming increasingly available.

If you work in the medical, mental health, care-giver or medical staff support industries, there is a huge opportunity here to make up the gaps in coverage and support by using AI.

Being involved in the discovery and decision-making groups in your industry, union, or organization could also give you a valuable advantage in an ever-changing industry. Though historically the medical industry is slow to change, AI will be increasing the speed of change and the adoption of AI will be increased by having it embedded into the technologies and vendors medical organizations are already using.

Key Takeaways From Chapter 6

AI can enhance healthcare: by automating repetitive tasks, creating more efficient communication and staffing levels, and helping with research and drug discovery. This leads to improved patient care, lower costs per patient, and helps in addressing the global shortage of skilled medical workers.

Augmenting medical professionals with AI tools: can lead to improved patient outcomes and serve more patients without necessarily increasing staff levels. Staff can be redirected to other tasks better suited to their skills, or be retrained to other career paths in a medical field which is already short staffed.

Proactive involvement in AI for staff: will be crucial for healthcare professionals to stay ahead in an industry poised for rapid transformation due to AI. Workers augmented by AI tools, robots, or other automation systems will each replace several workers unfamiliar with the technology.

CHAPTER 7: FINANCIAL SERVICES, TRADING, AND CONSULTING

It is 2025 and you open your phone to check your banking and investment accounts. You get a text from a friend to check out a company stock you hadn't heard of before.

You click the "call advisor" button and GPT-Angela answers.

"Have you heard of this new stock for a company called the U.S. Robots and Mechanical Men Corporation?" you ask.

GPT-Angela smiles and says, "It is good to see you again. I will look into that for you, please allow me a few seconds to gather the information."

"Take your time," you say, as you sip your morning beverage.

In a few seconds, she appears on the phone screen again. In front of her on the desk now are a number of papers and file folders.

GPT-Angela states cheerfully, "Thank you for waiting. The U.S. Robots and Mechanical Men Corporation has been making significant headlines recently. They are primarily known for their advancements in robotics and autonomous systems."

She pauses to shuffle the papers in front of her, picking up a newspaper, "Their stock price has surged in the past few days, largely due to a news story where one of their robots, designed for construction assistance, saved a co-worker's life during a hazardous situation at a construction site. Do you want to know more?"

You raise an eyebrow, intrigued, "Tell me more about this incident."

GPT-Angela adjusts her glasses, "Certainly. The incident took place last week at a skyscraper construction site. A heavy steel beam was accidentally dislodged from its place, and it was about to fall onto a worker below. The company's robot, operating nearby, detected the danger and moved the worker out of the way, preventing what could have been a fatal accident. This showcases the company's sophisticated AI capabilities and their robot's real-time decision-making skills. They are receiving a lot of media coverage for this story."

You nod, "That sounds impressive. But is this stock surge just a reaction to this news, or is there more underlying potential for this company?"

GPT-Angela flips through one of the folders, "The recent event certainly played a role in drawing attention to the company. However, U.S. Robots and Mechanical Men Corporation has a track record of innovative advancements in the field of robotics. They have been securing patents, partnering with AI companies, and investing heavily in research and development. Their robots are gaining traction in various industries, not just construction. Their healthcare and service robots are also receiving favorable reviews."

You ponder for a moment, "So, do you think this stock is a good long-term investment?"

GPT-Angela leans forward, "The robotics sector is predicted to grow exponentially in the next decade. U.S. Robots and Mechanical Men Corporation, given their innovative edge and strategic alliances, seems poised to be a key player in this growth. However, as with any investment, there are risks involved.

Considering the way your portfolio is diversified, I think that this would be a safe investment for you."

You smile, "Thank you, GPT-Angela. Let's move $1000 from my savings into this stock."

GPT-Angela nods, and then blinks her eyes for a few seconds.
"I have moved $1000 from your savings account into your trading account and I have made the stock purchase. I have sent a copy of the receipt to your inbox. By the way, your credit card payment for account 1234 is due in 8 days. Would you like me to make that payment for you now?"

"Yes, might as well, but schedule it for Friday," you reply.

"Your payment is scheduled. If you have any more questions, don't hesitate to reach out 24 hours a day, 7 days a week. Take care and have a great day!"

What Finance AI Systems Will Look Like

This interaction is fictional, of course, but the technology to make this work already exists. There are still a few pieces of the puzzle that need to be integrated to make it work. And there are also a few regulatory hurdles to ensure privacy and compliance. But this is not some far-off science fiction, all the tech needed is here now.

Imagine an AI system that knows all the regulations for the entire country, including every region, county, or district when it comes to financial transactions. It knows every bank, every stock, all the news and financial statements for every company for all of recorded history.

A system that is trained on all the financial vehicles and projections. It knows all the retirement strategies, investment strategies, and understands risk and reward with statistical accuracy.

This is already being built by several financial services firms. Analysts in several large Fintech companies already have access to "chat with documents" about every service and instrument their company offers.

The next step will be chatbots. Fewer support staff will be needed to field questions as the AI can handle more complex questions and as it gets more access to company data to answer customer inquiries.

Like online banking reduced the need for bank tellers by nearly 25%, AI chatbots will reduce support and customer service staff even further in financial sectors and banking.

In the 1970s and 80s, the invention of the Automatic Teller Machine spelled the end of bank tellers. Similar to the arguments that self-checkout would remove all cashier jobs. Of course, neither was the case and there are still bank tellers and there are still cashiers.

With ATMs, there was actually an increase in jobs, because banks used the savings to open more branches and this, in turn, ended up creating more jobs than were lost.

With self checkout, it is impossible to say exactly how many jobs were lost, but declines in retail workforce have been happening for two decades now. In the USA alone, more than 140,000 retail jobs have been lost - mostly due to online shopping.

The Uncanny Valley

But some people refuse to use self-checkout. Some people don't want to use the ATM. They want to talk to a person, and though a digital avatar may look and sound like a person, it is not a person.

And we are a ways off from having digital avatars which are indistinguishable from humans. The "uncanny valley" effect happens when we see things which are seemingly human, but not quite right. As avatars improve, the closer they get to humans, the more likely people will interact with them.

Coined by the Japanese roboticist Masahiro Mori in 1970, the Uncanny Valley refers to a dip in the positive emotional response people have to simulated humans. Something human-like but not too human-like seems endearing, and something indistinguishable from a human has a positive emotional effect. The dip is between those two, when we encounter something almost - but not quite human.

The primary reason for this effect, as proposed by Mori, is that the almost-lifelike object seems eerily "dead" or "zombielike" and evokes the same kind of revulsion as does a corpse.

There are also those who are wary of computers in general. They have seen mistakes in the past or were told of financial ruin due to computer error. They will avoid digital avatars just as they would rather hand their money to a bank teller, or give a credit card number over the phone, even though those transactions are way more likely to have mistakes, theft, or other issues.

AI will be used extensively in fraud detection and looking at patterns which may predict issues like fraud. It will also be used to try to detect things like insider trading, but stock price prediction is something already being tested with LLM systems.

Microtrading, Markets, and Prediction

In a recent study involving sentiment analysis of news articles for specific stocks, essentially looking for positive or negative news about or from each company, the findings were very interesting. (Linking GPT-4 Sentiment Analysis to Stock Price)

I asked ChatGPT-4 to help me summarize the findings and this is what I received back.

While GPT-4 sentiment scores exhibited some predictive

power, the accuracy was not consistent enough to guarantee profitable trading strategies in a real-world setting. Market noise, other news sources, and various macroeconomic factors play a significant role in stock price movements, making it challenging to rely solely on sentiment scores.

It seems that it is not about to guarantee profitable trading but it was able to show that there is promise that sentiment analysis, if combined with other market information, may allow companies to use AI to trade profitably with very little risk soon.

A more powerful AI, provided with real time data, could theoretically make trades and amass huge fortunes by predicting the trading activity of humans who lag behind in their ability to make decisions and follow trends.

Stock trading is not a zero-sum game. An AI could trade futures and other traders and the people creating the goods traded could all benefit from an increase in price, though eventually it is the consumer who pays for the increase. I am not an economist, but from my research, this seems to be the case.

There are a lot of ways this could go wrong. For example, a company using an AI trading system may be able to manipulate market sentiment through media and other means and "short" stocks or cause volatility in markets. I won't go further into this topic, but you can imagine how that would not be good.

Mortgages and Lending

The problem with lending is that it is essentially a calculation of many factors. The reason that deep learning systems are not used on the front lines of lending is because there are so many factors to consider.

Often there are "gut decisions" made by humans in underwriting or lending when dealing with people who don't easily fall into the existing formulae.

AI is very good at processing and analyzing huge amounts of data, but can also handle most of what we would consider "outliers" in the lending market. There are very few cases where someone or a company is looking for financing and is so far out of the box that an AI would not understand their situation.

The problem here is the same as with the rest of the financial sector. An AI chatbot, and eventually an avatar, can be created to replace some of the lenders and underwriters. When the process of lending is essentially collecting data, processing data, doing calculations, and handling communication, modern AI systems are extremely good at all of these functions.

However, as we learned earlier, many people will not trust "a computer" to handle the biggest financial transactions of their lives. They will want a person to talk to. A "real" human being who can tell them they understand, who can empathize, who can look at their situation and say, "we need to word this a certain way" or "we need to spin this a bit" to get the best chance of approvals.

Eventually an AI system will be able to handle these transactions, but there is also very little available training data on how the human parts of these interactions happen. No training data means you can't teach the system to do these things.

I believe that there will be a quick adoption of internal AI systems for financial services and consulting firms. Internal systems require fewer worries in the areas of privacy and compliance. Companies and employees who embrace these systems to improve their productivity will quickly surpass the abilities of non-AI users in their industry.

The Consultant of Advisor Role is Changing

There was a study about adding AI tools and training to business consultants. It was done by several brilliant folks, one of which is Ethan Mollick, who I had the pleasure of listening to on stage at

MAIcon in 2023. The results were quite striking.

> *For each one of a set of 18 realistic consulting tasks within the frontier of AI capabilities, consultants using AI were significantly more productive (they completed 12.2% more tasks on average, and completed tasks 25.1% more quickly), and produced significantly higher quality results (more than 40% higher quality compared to a control group).*

If you want to stay up to date on AI adoption and use, follow Ethan Mollick. He posts a lot of Twitter/X and LinkedIn and he's running dozens of experiments with dozens of AI systems.

Consultants and advisors can do more accurate work, more quickly than ever... If they are augmenting their abilities with AI. If you were to imagine a long running race, like a marathon, and one of the runners was 25.1% faster than the other runners, she would complete it half an hour before the next fastest competitor.

The gains from augmenting your tasks with AI are going to give you an insurmountable advantage over competitors if you work as a consultant or advisor. As the AI adoption curve increases, and more people in your industry are using AI, the advantage of starting to use it will become less striking. So the sooner you take advantage of AI systems, the better. And the investment by financial firms into their own AI systems is proof of their belief in this idea.

Being a Consultant means different things to different industries, but most often a consultant is there to solve a problem or improve a system. The ability to have discussions with a well trained AI specific to their industry will give consultants invaluable insight at a moment's notice.

With the ability to help improve systems, processes, structures, and procedures, based on all the available instrusty experience and research, and to have it already educated with every book ever written on the subject, will make them able to more easily direct businesses.

Unfortunately, an AI with this ability will soon be able to surpass the average consultant or advisor who doesn't have some kind of experience or wisdom not contained in a format that can be used for training data. When knowledge is not documented, it will be unavailable to AI. (At least until the invention of AGI)

The Trust Factor

When people are entrusting their retirement, their ability to purchase a home, or the future of their businesses to someone, they will want that someone to be a human being.

However, it won't be long before the humans we trust to help us need to be ones who are effectively using AI.

If they are not augmenting their jobs with AI, they will not be chosen by us as consumers or prospects because they will be unable to meet the bar of our minimum expectations.

People may not trust AI, but they also are being given advice by their peers. Our peers will refer people to us who have given them outstanding results. They will refer us to their financial advisor who is bringing in returns that outpace the market. It is unlikely in the near future that these top performers will be working without the aid of several AI systems.

These AI-augmented advisors and consultants will far surpass their peers and will be referred to more often, be able to work with more clients in the same amount of time, and will be able to out-earn their non-AI-using counterparts.

Key Takeaways From Chapter 7

The Future of Financial AI Systems: The envisioned future of financial AI systems, as depicted in the interaction with GPT-Angela, showcases the integration of banking, investment advice, and timely notifications. Such systems can comprehensively manage financial information, ensuring compliance and understanding of complex regulations. As these systems advance, they will likely lead to reductions in customer service staff in the financial sectors, similar to the decline of bank tellers with the advent of online banking.

AI in Trading and Consulting: The integration of AI in stock trading, sentiment analysis, and microtrading presents potential advantages and challenges. While AI can potentially predict and capitalize on trading trends faster than humans, there are concerns about manipulating market sentiment. In the realm of consulting, AI augmentation can significantly boost productivity and quality of results. Consultants leveraging AI will have a distinct advantage over their peers, making them more efficient and knowledgeable.

The Trust Factor and the Role of AI-Augmented Advisors: Despite the capabilities of AI, the "uncanny valley" effect and general mistrust in machines for significant financial decisions indicate that humans still seek a personal touch. However, the most trusted human advisors in the near future will likely be those who effectively use AI to enhance their decision-making. These AI-augmented professionals will outpace their peers, delivering better results and earning more referrals.

CHAPTER 8: TRANSPORTATION, LOGISTICS, AGRICULTURE, MANUFACTURING, AND SELF DRIVING

I was in Toronto, Ontario, Canada, for the "Zoholics" conference, a company-specific conference for people using the AI-powered software *Zoho* to manage their businesses. But that's not the important bit.

I want to talk to you about the Uber ride I took to the airport.

We all know the story of ridesharing taking over taxis, but I want to remind you that taxis still exist. But this is also an important personal story of someone I met who was directly affected by the change in the taxi industry. It will illuminate the change in cost to doing business when an industry is disrupted with automation and AI.

My rideshare driver was excited - or overly caffeinated, hard to tell. But he was a former cab driver turned rideshare driver, who had just purchased a townhome in a seriously price-inflated housing market in the largest metropolitan area in Canada.

We talked a bit about housing prices and rental units and he mentioned, "When I moved to Canada I worked two jobs and saved every penny. Then when I started my own cab business, I had two choices, buy a cab license or buy a house. The cab license was almost three hundred thousand dollars."

"Holy smokes!" I said, though the word I used was a little more profane.

"Now I don't even drive a cab, just rideshare and deliveries. By the time I sold [the cab license], it was worth less than one hundred thousand. I should have bought the house because now the same house is worth 1.2 Million."

I looked up the costs of Cab licenses in Toronto, and I discovered that at the highest point it was $360,000 in mid 2012. As Uber came to town in March 2012 in Toronto, the cost then plummeted to $100,000 average in 2014.

In 2022, a cab license was just $676.22.

When an automated system "comes to town," the price of working in the industry is drastically lowered. In this case, when Uber arrived in Toronto, the cost of doing business dropped by more than 50%. When the cost of entry is reduced, more players join the game to compete.

By the time there were multiple ridesharing competitors all working against Taxis in the same market, the cost of doing business had reduced by 99.8% where licenses were concerned. Everyone left holding the licenses couldn't sell them unless it was at an absolute loss. Many drivers just turned in their licenses and refused the renewal cost. Most went to drive for rideshare companies.

If you look at the cost reduction from industrialization, to automation and robotics, the cost per unit in every industry plummets. The barrier to entry is lowered (excluding regulatory capture, but that's for another chapter).

The incumbents in the industry are often surprised at how quickly their industry is commoditized or replaced. Even though in hindsight, we can see all the signs that spelled their downfall, at the time, most of the people in the industries did not see it coming, just like my Uber-driver who "should have bought the house."

Automation in Manufacturing and Agriculture is Old News

Most manufacturing has been somewhat automated for decades now. I have a couple of clients who do manufacturing and their manufacturing floors have almost no employees. The ones they do have are generally working on the machines themselves, to ensure they are running or re-tooling them for a different part they are making. Most of their staff are administrative, sales, support, and warehouse staff.

The assembly line worker of the past is already in short supply in most manufacturing industries. Offshoring, robotics, and automation have been leveraged by corporations to reduce the majority of these blue-collar jobs. And just like half of the US workforce was once in farming, but now only 1.4% of the US workforce is in agriculture, other industries will have similar reductions in workforce.

But the jobs that do exist are often because the job is considered, "too complex to be automated." Or that the position requires too much on-the-spot decision making. For example, farmers often bring in farm labor - let's say, to pick apples. Or an injection molding company might have staff working on "assembly and finishing" which is where parts are put together, maybe screws or springs are added, decals, paint, etc.

These jobs are often finicky and require fine motor skills. They also require staff to be able to change the execution of their tasks slightly depending on manufacturing defects or subtle differences. Our fruit picking labor needs to make a decision on if the apple is ripe or if it has blemishes and isn't ready for sale.

Robot See; Robot Do

The problem with the arguments people use to say an AI can't take their job is that they boil down to the idea that a robot can't "see" things.

Robots have the fine motor skills to do any human task, just look at surgical robots. In fact, robots can handle tasks which require extreme precision. Depending on the robot and the use case, it could be precise to amounts smaller than a human eye can detect.

Optics combined with AI will allow these systems to see, make decisions, and take actions. Most large language model AI systems already understand the language Scratch, used in robotics, as well as C++ and other computer languages associated with programming the robots.

There are also existing robots who can be taught tasks by showing them how to accomplish them rather than programming the steps to accomplish the task. This allows diversity in the way that tasks are completed.

MIT's Computer Science and Artificial Intelligence Laboratory (CSAIL) have developed systems like RoboTurk which allow humans to show or guide robot training in real time. Robot see, robot do.

Robots can also be trained by using a technique called multi-agent reinforcement training. If one robot knows the task, the other robots also know the task. That way, if your company has several robot arms at different facilities, you only need to train one of them to train them all.

This can be more efficient than training people because you need to either get all the people in the same place to train them, or they require training manuals, online courses, video training or other methods, all of which could train an AI-powered robot as well. If those materials exist, that training would be quick and cheap.

These more powerful robots can use optics to see and learn a task But they are adaptable to variations and even improvise to a certain extent. The more one learns, the more they all learn.

> *"To succeed, planning alone is insufficient. One must improvise as well." - Isaac Asimov, Foundation*

It is very Borg-like, to make a Star Trek reference. And once general purpose robots are available, the labor market could be in a lot of trouble. Fortunately, there is a lot of time before that happens.

However, there are instances where these systems are already integrated into existing technology. For example, there is an automated agricultural solution made by Israeli startup, Tevel Aerobotics Technologies. The fruit-picking system uses drones to fly into trees, analyze each apple for ripeness and quality and then pick (or not pick) the ones that will go to market. They work with "swarm" programming, a term used when controlling multiple robots at once for efficiency.

These technologies are all pointing to a future where laborious tasks, even complex ones, can be done with the use of robotics or AI-powered autonomous devices like drones. It will take decades before "the robots" are made to work in nearly all environments or within all industry sectors. If the current trajectory of these advances continues, then "manual labor" will be reduced over time at a consistently declining rate.

There is now only 1.4% of the USA workforce in agriculture, there will be a similar decline in labor, and the cost of labor will be reduced in a way similar to the cost reduction in taxicab licenses.

Imagine a future where we have robots building robots. Where the AI systems team up with humans to incrementally improve those robots and the systems they use to create themselves. This will further improve the effectiveness of those robots while driving the cost down. No human will be able to compete with robot labor in 20 or 30 years on a cost per unit of output basis.

Steering Clear of Humans: Robots Hit the Road

Self Driving has been talked about and tested for decades now, but the biggest advancements have happened in the last couple of years.

In long-haul trucking, the advantages for the industry seem to be pretty clear cut.

The American Trucking Association estimates that the industry has a shortfall of 80,000 drivers now, and even though there has been a decrease in demand since interest rates increased in 2022, there is still a large shortfall.

Generally speaking, autonomous long-haul trucking would go from one facility to another, outside of urban areas.Some states will require a "driver" to be in the vehicle while others require only one driver per three vehicles (when those trucks travel together).

Estimates by the Boston Consulting Group (BCG) expect that fully autonomous vehicles would save 30% on labor costs and maintenance. Because vehicles can stay in service without breaks for drivers, they would have less downtime. Staying on the road instead of pulling off for food and bathroom breaks, more consistent driving, and other efficiencies could save 10-15% of emissions and fuel costs.

This reduction in staff would also reduce the backlog of hiring drivers. Though drivers would still be needed for certain situations, driving into urban environments, and other factors, this is just one piece of the long-haul trucking puzzle which could help solve the current labor shortfall.

That said, this could contribute to lower wages for drivers, because things less in demand tend to cost less. Also, there have been negative actions taken against self-driving vehicles and industry changes, like negative salary expectations, could cause violence or interference with autonomous vehicles.

In San Francisco in 2023, Safe Street Rebel, an anti-autonomous car community, waged a war on self-driving vehicles. They are disabling them by simply placing an orange traffic cone on the hood. This stops the vehicle from being able to "see" and the vehicle will put on its hazard lights and wait to be "enabled" again by having the cone removed from its front hood or until a company employee shows up to reset the vehicle's safety system.

Though a lot of promise has been shown with Fully Self-Driving vehicles (FSD) they are still a long way from being driverless in every situation. Though autonomous vehicles have passed nearly a half billion miles of self-driving, they cannot deal with every possible situation. They are also mostly tested in positive-weather situations.

I can tell you from driving in Nova Scotia that there is stuff coming at you continuously that isn't common in San Francisco. From birds flying in my car window, mixes of snow, salt water, and ice on roads, "pea soup" fog, deer, porcupines, skunks, foxes, and even the odd beaver on the road, I don't think FSD cars are ready for everywhere.

If you consider trucking routes in the warmer parts of the USA, or that only run in fair-weather conditions, the idea of long haul trucking using FSD is not that much of a stretch. Especially when you consider that there are several thousand self-driving vehicles already driving roads in the USA for testing. You may have driven past an FSD vehicle and not known it.

Another option for self-driving vehicles is to use the technology the military uses when driving drones. This way a trucking company could have drivers "on-hand" in real time with their trucks, available to take over if needed remotely. These vehicles would disable themselves if the remote driver is not available. Similar to the way driverless cars stop when a traffic cone is placed on their hood to block their cameras and sensors.

It may be a long time before FSD is available to all types of driving. But it will come to the "low hanging fruit" of the industry first and that is small areas with fair weather, or long-haul trucking routes which do not need to go into more dangerous areas like urban freeways and downtown streets.

The Drive-Thru Meets the Driverless Car

Once we have full self driving, you will talk to your car to tell it what you want. There won't be a need for you to be in it to get things done.

For example, if your car knows you are going to get up for work at 7am, and leave at 7:45am, it can do the following.

1. Check the traffic and charge level of the car. Check the weather. Estimate the distances and times for your commute.
2. Order your Latte from Starbucks and your Breakfast Burrito from Don Pedro's and then go pick them up for you.
3. The drive-thru window already has your order ready and the car opens the door to let the employee place it in the car for you.
4. The car's internal camera sees that the coffee is placed in the drink holder and the bag on the seat. Feeling it is secure it adds a tip to your order and pays with your card on file.

5. Your car comes back to pick you up and ensures the seat position and temperature are perfect for your preferences.
6. "Hello, your coffee and breakfast are ready. Shall we proceed to work?"
7. Drives you safely to work.
8. Drives out of the downtown core to a place where parking is free. It estimates the time needed to pick you up and comes back for you when you're done work.

This may seem like science fiction, but it's not too far off.

What does this do to ride sharing drivers when I can have my car drive me around when I need it, without me needing to be in charge?

And we already know from various legal battles and data leaks from ridesharing companies and FSD companies that they all have at least considered plans to replace the rideshare and delivery fleets of drivers with autonomous vehicles. Self driving ride sharing could also be trained to handle complex scenarios like the one above using modern AI language models.

Make no mistake about it. If you drive rideshare, deliver packages or food, or transport goods, someone somewhere is working on replacing your job with AI automation.

The only question is how long it will take. Residential delivery, inner-city trucking, and other use cases could be pretty far off. But self-driving airport shuttles, long-haul trucking, and even food delivery will begin to have human labor replaced by AI before the end of 2025.

There may be regulatory hurdles, legal challenges, and human backlash, but the cost savings and efficiencies will eventually outweigh the ability of those systems to resist the people backing the technologies.

For better or for worse, FSD will be here soon and it's only going to get more functional and hopefully, safer.

The Ghost in the Supply Chain

According to McKinsey, the biggest optimization for supply chains will be centered around the idea of an AI-based "control tower." The system that monitors the entire process from end to end.

Each part of the process will have its own integrations and possibly AI-based systems to help control pricing based on improved insights into demand analysis, price forecasting for raw materials, agile production planning and scheduling, and helping to manage risk.

The other big advantage will be shipping logistics and distribution. An AI-system can read the endless flow of data in real time and help find ways to optimize the entire logistical chain from sourcing to last mile delivery. Optimizing routing, freight contracting, vessel or container sharing, are all on the table.

These types of optimization aren't just good for reducing costs, but they also reduce environmental impact.

As ports and other types of logistical work get more automated, there will be less demand for the "labor" type of work we are used to seeing. The forklift driver or other machine operator, will likely be replaced eventually by computer vision and AI.

Self driving isn't just for cars. It means forklifts, cranes, trucking, and other parts of the logistical framework that runs the economy. Companies and governments alike are looking to reduce costs and to keep the flow of goods moving if there is another pandemic or shutdown.

Let alone the reluctance these organizations often have in working with unions. In the eyes of the pure capitalist or the bureaucrat, unions are a cost, not a benefit. The automated machines of logistics will most likely be installed and managed by vendors – which means, most likely non-unionized workers.

I am all for collective bargaining, but in an industry where human labor is being made obsolete, I fear that the need to organize labor will be lost.

Jobs which will increase are the installation and maintenance of these types of machines. There will always need to be a few people on the ground to ensure things run smoothly and deal with problems, but the workforce reduction has already started and will slowly continue as automation is increased.

If there are fewer laborers, there will be fewer supervisors, less HR and hiring personnel, less management, and so on. The cascade will go down the line. But this is not going to happen as swiftly as other industries.

When it comes to shipping, automation has already reduced the workers in these industries.

The average container ship carries thousands of goods across the ocean and generally speaking has a crew of 20 or less people. There were more crew on a pirate ship in the 1800s. Some of them had as many as 200 "staff" on board.

The machines used in shipping ports, freight shipping, warehouses, and other types of logistics facilities are often large, and can be dangerous. The amount of testing involved and the time it takes to change regulations will make this a slow process. But to be completely honest with you, in my opinion, if you work in logistics and your employer offers an early retirement package, take it. I'm not a financial planner and this is not to be considered financial advice. My fear for you is that this might be the best retirement package you will ever get. Once the writing's on the wall for everyone to see, they will have more leverage to give you less.

If you are not anywhere near retirement, I would consider trying to work yourself into the more complex parts of the logistics business. The harder a task is to learn, and the less written and video recordings of how a process works, the better, because it will be harder to train the AI-powered equipment to take those jobs.

Key Takeaways From Chapter 8

Ridesharing Impact: Ridesharing platforms, powered by AI, have significantly impacted traditional taxi services, highlighting the broader implications of automation in transportation.

Robot Adaptability: Advanced robots, with AI capabilities, can adapt to tasks, learn from variations, and even improvise, suggesting a potential shift in the labor market.

Autonomous Logistics: Autonomous logistics, driven by AI, promise advanced vehicles that cater to personalized user preferences, reshaping the way we interact with and experience transportation.

CHAPTER 9: EDUCATION AND RESEARCH

First off, let's put the worst idea to bed right now.

There is no "AI detection tool" that has a statistically significant way of detecting AI created content. You will be able to detect watermarks and metadata, but all those things can be modified by anyone with even basic technical skills.

Trying to detect "cheating" with AI is a futile pursuit. All that educational institutions do by trying to detect AI use is create better cheaters.

I wholeheartedly believe that we need to encourage our students to learn to embrace AI. They need to be comfortable with how to use it and have the experience working with a variety of AI systems. If not, someone else will. And our youth will be woefully unprepared for the future.

The Writing Is On The Wall

Over the next 36 months, AI is poised to notably impact education.

In most educational institutions, from public school to colleges and universities, it can sometimes seem that change happens at a slower pace than some of us would like.

But I think the combination of the pandemic lockdowns and the sudden appearance of publicly available generative AI has thrust educators into a future they never expected.

- Fostering personalized learning experiences
- Developing intelligent tutoring systems
- Streamlining administrative tasks
- Providing predictive analytics to help guide our students
- Empowering our educators with data analysis tools
- Creative tools to create new learning resources

I think one of the most telling comparative graphs I saw online recently was that the traffic to minecraft servers went down and the traffic to OpenAI increased at almost an identical rate when the kids went back to school. I honestly don't know if that was a real statistic, but it is humorous at least to think that is the case.

My daughter grew up in a world much different than my own, and not just because we had her when I was already in my 40s. Since she can remember, devices understand when you talk to them, at least a basic level.

She can tell Alexa to play music, or ask daddy to "Use the AI to make a coloring page for me."

"What would you like to color?" I ask her.

"A baby dragon… Oh! And a Kitty."

My daughter has grown up with the ability to generate any image she can imagine to color or to use in her artwork. She's seven, and she's already ahead of the curve compared to most people on the planet when it comes to using AI.

This brings up a problem and an opportunity.

As I have said before, "the future is already here, it's just not evenly distributed." A quote usually attributed to William Gibson but no one seems to be sure.

Students in countries who don't have Internet access available, families in remote communities who don't have satellite internet, children who don't have devices to use the Internet with, all have the same problem. No AI for them. At least, until some day when we're handing out AI-Powered laptops.

Those countries and school systems who block the use of the most powerful foundational AI models for whatever reason, no matter how noble, are robbing their children of the chance to work with the most powerful systems. The most capable artificially intelligent systems will be invisible cut off from them.

Meanwhile, the children who do have access will learn faster. They will quickly learn the idea that we augment our capacity for productivity, for learning, for creativity, and for fun, with the technology that is available to us.

Imagine kids now, not learning to use a computer or a tablet? They would be so far behind their peers when it comes to opportunities. Many a science fiction tale has been woven about those who can't make the cut, because they never had the digital augmentation of their peers, usually relegated to the shanty towns of a dystopian future.

But who's to say the AI system will work for teaching kids faster? Who's to say they will even be aligned with the goals of humanity? Well they won't be, if our next generation doesn't even understand how to work with them.

We are handing the reins of AI over to the kids and young adults. They are the hundreds huddled in the Llama Lounge in San Francisco building the apps of the future. They are the one who will grow up with AI in everything, just like their parents always had the Internet, and just like my parents always had color TV and telephones, and so on.

The generation who grows up with the technology are the ones who figure out the second act. They build the next layer in

technology, culture, and how society integrates with that tech. It would behoove us to prepare them as best we can.

I will step down from my soapbox now. Agree with me or not, AI is here. And according to a Pew research study, the youth and the most educated and wealthy among us are the ones who are more likely to be using AI.

If our school systems don't start teaching AI and how to use these systems, at least at a basic level, then the distribution of the knowledge will be resting with the most affluent and the children of those who are already well educated. I fear that the children in some rural areas, those with families of less means, immigrants, and marginalized communities could fall even further behind the educational curve - and the opportunities others will be able to take advantage of.

Policy and Progress

Schools need to start to solve for AI now. Less than 14% of US school systems have any AI policy at all for students. And less than 5% have a policy for children.

School systems in New York City and Boston have already adopted policies around generative AI and allow its use when instructed by teachers, and credit when it has been used in a project. The policy also helps to govern the use of AI by faculty.

The important part here is to have a policy. Having nothing means anything goes. It also means that punishment for perceived AI use will be unevenly distributed across the school systems. Studies on AI detection systems found that they often penalize non-native English speakers. This means minorities are more likely to be impacted by punishment for AI use, even when they may not have used an AI program in their assignements.

What Steps Can You Take?

The most important parts are forming a policy framework for AI and Generative AI in your organization. Specifically for education systems, the process can look something like this.

1. **You Need a Team**: Find others in your organization interested in or those with a basic understanding of AI. These are your AI champions. Meet first. Then you want to create a list of others you can bring in over time. Admins, teachers, students, parents, outside experts, and possibly even the school's or school board's legal counsel, eventually.

2. **Set Some Goals:** When are you going to provide a policy draft. Who will see it. Do people need to vote on it? Who is doing what, and when.

3. **Find the Others:** Who is already doing this and what has been their experience so far. Will they allow you to copy their policy as a framework for your own?

4. **Your Policy Draft:** This is the guidelines around AI use, AI ethics, which systems to use, and how systems are evaluated. You may need more than one policy if they are for students, teachers, or administrative staff.

5. **Get Input and Finalize:** Get the input you need from all the layers in the organization that need to have input. The more transparent you are in the process, the more easily it will be approved and adopted.

6. **Educate:** Ensure that everyone has access to and understands the policy. Determine how training and policy changes will be delivered to students, to faculty, the public, and to the organization as a whole.

Once you have a policy in place, your organization can move forward without ambiguity on policy. Students and teachers will know what is acceptable.

And remember that if you are one of the pioneers of this project, it looks great on your CV, but also it can help to galvanize you against future cuts. Especially if those cuts are related to AI. You don't lay off the AI policy team when you are planning to use more AI. (*I mean the could, but that would be a bit short sighted.*)

What Do You Done Once You Have a Policy

Now your entire organization can look at where they can benefit from AI systems. This could be in administrative and documentation tasks, creating assignments, improving curriculum, or advancing learning programs.

You can find the tasks that are repetitive or redundant and use AI to help automate those tasks. AI can help with communication to parents and writing grant applications.

It can help students learn more about subjects and ask questions they have in a safe environment, without having to feel the pressure of asking questions in front of their peers.

If you don't create a policy, some students and staff are going to use it anyway... And there will be no way to catch them. It is ludicrous to believe that banning something you can't detect is a good idea.

Especially when programs like Grammarly or Blue Pencil have generative AI built into their spelling and grammar checkers, and they are directly marketing to students. Good luck with that to those who try.

The myriad of ways to use AI in schools is far too large a subject for this book, but I imagine we will soon see the use cases.

AI and Research

One of those use cases is research, as we mentioned, but I am also talking about medical research, physics, chemistry, biology, and all the college and doctorate level research from MIT to NSCC in Nova Scotia. AI will be in the lab and the classroom.

In the evolving landscape of research, Artificial Intelligence has already played a pivotal role by augmenting the capabilities of researchers to discover new drugs, new drug combinations, and to analyze huge data sets related to medical conditions.

Another way AI is helpful is in predictive analysis since the generative AI programs are based on predictions in the first place. In physics it helps in simulating complex systems. In chemistry, AI-driven tools are being employed for molecular design and to unravel the complexities of chemical reactions, while in biology, it is aiding in genomic sequencing and understanding cellular processes.

The integration of AI doesn't stop at the lab. Everything from grant writing to helping to write our results can be assisted. The administrative benefits for research labs with sometimes limited budgets can mean spending more on equipment or staff and spending less of their time and resources on non-research duties.

Furthermore, AI's capability to handle massive datasets is indispensable in contemporary research. The ability to sift through unimaginable amounts of data, identifying patterns and extracting valuable insights, significantly accelerates the research process.

Author's Note: The compute needed for AI is being built now, with billions of dollars in investment.

The supercomputers of the past used in research, could handle petaflops of data. That is one thousand trillion calculations per second. Modern AI systems run on clusters of servers using vector processessors (originally made for video games and 3D modeling) and are measured in exaflops. Or a million trillion floating point calculations per second. 1 exaflop == 1,000 petaflops.

Anthropics' new AI cluster is going to be ten million times more calculations per second than the modern exoflop systems. It should come online in 2024. The number of calculations is so large that no name was assigned to that much computing power when the standard naming index was invented.

The ability to have this much processing power and to analyze massive amounts of data at a time is particularly beneficial in interdisciplinary research endeavors where the amalgamation of insights from different fields can lead to groundbreaking discoveries.

AI also fosters collaboration across geographical and disciplinary boundaries. Researchers from diverse fields and regions can work together on shared platforms, powered by AI, to solve complex problems. They don't need to speak the same language or even know one another as the AI will be able to coordinate the research on their behalf.

This collaborative ethos is likely to drive innovation at an unprecedented scale, transcending traditional barriers that once impeded the free flow of ideas.

One of the benefits often overlooked by people who are not in technical fields is the ability to use AI to help create software and automation. You may be familiar with the idea of low-code or no-code software, where you can use a computer program to write another program without being a programmer. This can help you do calculations, manipulate or move data, gather input from study subjects, make websites, develop surveys, and so on.

AI development tools will be able to write code "on the fly" or assist in developing programs you need to do specific tasks. Because of the nature of AI to give you different responses with each query, you may need something that takes specific standardized actions every time. For example, I want my mortgage calculator to give me the same, correct result every time

I use it and I don't really need an essay about how mortgages work.

You will be able to ask your AI to develop a program that asks for a certain input, does some kind of data manipulation, and then gives you a certain output. The AI will write the program for you. In fact, this is how the current ChatGPT-4 Advanced Data Analysis works. When you ask it to do something, it writes a Python program and then attempts to create the result you asked for.

There are many protocols and frameworks in development to allow AI programs to integrate with one another without any programming involved. Once these are functional, connecting your AI or AI-research assistant to data sources or other AI programs will be a trivial endeavor.

There even could be people who learn because they enjoy it. Imagine that! AI isn't going to replace them, and if there is some form of UBI (Universal Basic Income) in the future because of job losses, then a new culture of learning will arise. These future experts will be making discoveries because they want to - not for any commercial purpose. (as many are passionate about their own disciplines now)

Sometimes creativity in research isn't just a logic puzzle or a matter of analyzing a large enough data set. Sometimes it's happy mistakes, sometimes it is a crazy dream, or inspiration we get while we're in the shower.

Just because AI is working in research, even if it ends up taking over most research, there will still be more to discover that it is just not well designed to figure out.

Education Meets AI

In the coming years, the symbiotic relationship between AI and academia is poised to deepen. As AI continues to mature, its applications within research labs and classrooms are bound to proliferate, paving the way for a new era of discovery and learning.

The future holds promise of a symbiotic relationship where AI becomes an indispensable companion in the quest for knowledge, from the lab and the lecture hall. As long as we don't stifle the inevitable by trying to ban the use of AI in schools, which is as futile as past bans on smartphones and calculators.

I remember people screaming that the Internet was going to ruin education. Imagine that.

Key Takeaways From Chapter 9

Need for Embracing AI in Education: Matt emphasizes the importance of integrating AI in education, arguing that attempts to detect and curb AI usage only lead to better cheaters. By embracing AI, students become more familiar and comfortable with this burgeoning technology, preparing them for a future where AI will be everywhere.

AI's Impending Impact on Education and Research: In the next three years, AI is expected to significantly influence education by fostering personalized learning, streamlining administrative tasks, and enhancing research capabilities in higher education and in the lab. AI can accelerate research by handling massive datasets, aiding in predictive analysis, and fostering interdisciplinary collaborations.

Policy Framework Requirement: The author advocates for the development of clear policies regarding AI usage in educational institutions. Such policies will ensure fairness, clarity on AI usage, and will also avoid any ambiguous scenarios where AI might be used unethically. The proposed policy framework aims to guide the responsible use of AI, bringing along administrative and educational advancements, while also bridging the digital divide by making AI education accessible to a broader demographic.

CHAPTER 10: INFORMATION WORKERS, ADMINISTRATIVE, AND SALES

Information workers

By combining estimates from large consulting firms from the USA and Canada, I have arrived at a rough estimate of job losses for non-management information workers.

In my opinion, 20% of jobs from non-management information or digital workers are at risk in the next 36 months. This is an average. Some industries will fare better than others.

Imagine an administrative or information worker position. This could be the executive admin for a business unit, a coordinator, event planner, business analyst, project manager, technical writer, librarian, database admin... The list is too long to even scratch the surface here.

This employee does 80% repetitive time-consuming tasks (including meetings and coordination of those tasks) and only 20% of the tasks they do on a daily basis require a thinking, creative, human who can make decisions and build client relationships, etc.

Some of it could be all the "busy work", as some people call it, non-vital tasks to the organization. A lot of folks work on moving data from old systems to new systems, analyzing reports from non-integrated external systems, compiling data and analyzing it to build reports, putting together all the information about a project, documenting, assigning resources, and all the things that make businesses run.

There will be a few steps in the integration of AI into all industries, but especially for information workers. This process is accelerated by the massive amount of investments happening in AI by the biggest tech companies in the world.

Understanding the next few steps of how AI will be adopted and delivered to industry will allow you to see the future. In the next chapter, you will get the steps you can take to stay relevant in the Age of AI.

The First Step: Generative AI Integrations

Author's Note: We currently use or have used every tool mentioned in this first step at our marketing agency.

Staff could be using ChatGPT to help summarize data or write reports. It could be content creation tasks or repurposing content for marketing. It could be handling data analysis or doing research.

Maybe your marketing team is using RunwayML, Wonder Studio or GetMunch to handle video. Descript to edit podcasts and vodcasts. ChatGPT to translate transcripts. Eleven Labs or PlayHT to generate human-sounding voices.

Staff could be using Writer or Jasper to help with content creation, as well as writing documentation or instruction manuals. ChatGPT Advanced Data Analysis could be used to convert files, massage data, find insights, and create charts and graphs.

Maybe your information services or IT teams are using a generative AI system like Code Llama to help them write software or squash bugs more quickly. Help with automating systems, finding ways to harden IT security, or training staff on phishing scams.

Step Two: Integration of AI Into The Tools You Use Already

Microsoft Co-Pilot, Google Duet or Gemini, Zoho Zia, Teams, Slack, Salesforce, Hubspot, Grammarly, Workspace, etc. Every SaaS tool your company is using will have an AI built into it. And it's not going to take long.

If every tool doesn't have an AI component by mid 2024, I'd be shocked.

This is also the part where integrations start to work together. The initial round of "proof of concept" tools that were rushed to market but maybe aren't the most useful will be replaced by tools that solve specific business problems.

Tools will have access to your business communications, documents, and can help with summarizing meetings into notes, making more efficient data analysis, better spreadsheets, simpler integrations, and access to automation. It will be like everyone has an assistant as well as an entry-level developer as their personal staff.

Step 3: AI Agents

An AI-agent is a program that can create a plan, communicate with both people and software, and has the ability to handle tasks autonomously.

There are many different forms of AI-Agents already in

development.

Some AI-Agents are information-only, they can handle several prompts to another AI or other systems and then report their findings.

Another type of AI-Agent is called a multi-agent or multi-gen, which blends several autonomous AI-agents into one system. It runs much like an office would. There is a "boss agent" who creates and monitors the plan, like a project manager would. Then the other AI systems have their own tasks. One could be a software developer. One could be used to go get data and convert it into the form needed for the task. And so on.

The most likely future rendition is going to be the multi-agent model. These AI-Agents will be created to be industry specific.

Just like a construction company would buy an accounting program made to handle the construction industry, you would purchase or lease an AI-Agent made for the management of construction projects.

There will also be foundational-model agents (which may end up being named something else). This is the idea that the program is set up but isn't trained with any data yet. This would allow a business to bring the AI-Agent "in house" and train it on their own data.

Imagine that this AI-Agent is trained specifically for your business. It is trained on all the previously recorded calls from your customer service and support staff. It has all the knowledge base data, and has read every blog and article on your website, every press release, every training manual and HR guide.

It knows where all the company's documents are and the contents of each. It has been taught who is allowed access to which data. What data should be kept to internal staff, and what is OK to share with the public.

It knows all the latest news, weather, logistical data, stock prices, every order, every client... And it can be unleashed on all the repetitive tasks of your staff.

What Happens Next?

With some testing and tweaking, it will soon handle those 80% of the tasks that don't require a human, faster than a human ever could.

In fact, it will likely spend most of its time idle, waiting to be told what to do until the systems can be optimized to handle more tasks on their own without being told to do them. It has been the case for more than 20 years now that the bottleneck in most computer-based tasks is us entering the instructions or information.

Without being shackled by the arduous day to day tasks, you will be freed up to add more value to your business or organization. You can focus on the things that really make a difference. We all know that a lot of people spend too much time "working in the business and not working on the business."

But not everyone will see productivity gains the same way. There will be organizations who see a reduction in the tasks of their employees as a chance to reduce headcount and save money. This is why I predict that some jobs will be in jeopardy.

What About Sales?

The job of sales staff has already shifted substantially since the end of the twentieth century. The average buyer has way more information now, thanks to the Internet. An educated buyer has meant less sales staff and more marketing staff, ensuring that the prospects have the information they want before they contact sales.

I remember a time when people said no one would ever buy a car or a computer or any large purchase on the Internet. I actually worked in commission sales in the 90s. I remember when no one bought things online. They were afraid to!

Sales staff since then have been reduced substantially. According to the US Board of Labor Statistics. They predicted that salesperson jobs in the US are projected to decline by 2.3% by 2026. This will result in a loss of 101,900 jobs.

However, in corporate sales, I feel the salesperson will be freed from the work of documentation and administrative tasks that keep them from being "out there" making sales. This may lead to a more productive sales team which could benefit the company and reduce the chance of layoffs in their sector.

However, an army of well-trained AI-Agents who can video chat, or talk on the phone, where there is no delay or discernable way to tell the difference between them and a human being could end up taking a big bite out of the sales job market. Imagine AI sales agents who are trained from every sales interaction, able to incrementally improve their pitches and responses with each new interaction.

That is a way off though. Even though the technology is nearly there, we are entering the uncanny valley effect for video avatars. Digital people who seem human but just not quite right... They could turn off some buyers and make digital sales agents less effective if they are nearly, but not quite, human.

The human sales rep who can go out, shake hands, and have lunch with a prospect, or who can hit the golf course, do the lunch presentation, work the trade show booth, or have the "Ladies Lunch" will have an advantage over the AI-Agents for a while to come.

If you are in sales, think about what your human advantages are. And if you don't have any, then it's time to get some.

Key Takeaways From Chapter 10

Potential Job Losses and AI Integration: About 20% of non-management information jobs may be at risk in the next 36 months. Many workers spend as much as 80% of their time on tasks AI could potentially automate, emphasizing the need to focus on human-centric roles.

The Rise of AI Agents: AI -Agents, especially multi-agent models, will become industry-specific tools. They will handle tasks autonomously, possibly leading to job reductions in many industries and industry sectors.

Sales in the Age of AI: The sales role has evolved with more informed buyers. While AI can streamline sales tasks, human interaction remains a unique advantage in the sales domain.

CHAPTER 11: STAY RELEVANT IN THE AGE OF AI

Now that we understand some of the changes coming to industry, we need to know what to do about it.

If you skipped to the end, you are welcome to read through this but there may be examples from previous chapters and other industries that are relevant to your understanding of the topic. I highly recommend you read the entire book and have a well-rounded understanding of what will happen across industries.

Who Is Taking Whose Job?

In most cases in the next 12-36 months, your job is not directly in jeopardy from an AI, but rather a person who is using AI to be more productive.

In some cases, like technical support or customer service, if your job is primarily helping people over voice or text chat, your job is in direct jeopardy because of an AI-powered software program that is trained on all the details of the company; their products, policies, and customer orders.

I'm not going to blow smoke up your ass here. There are going to be some tough choices and some people are going to be treated unfairly.

114

Some folks who deserve to do well are going to get the ax. Nice people, with families to support, who work hard and are punctual and polite, will be replaced by automation. It is going to happen. Period.

Unless there is a massive social movement to replace capitalism, which I don't see happening in the next decade, then we need to deal with the reality of what is happening. I know we tend to blame the messenger, but keep in mind, I am just predicting what is going to happen so that you can try to have the best chance of staying employed or keeping your business afloat.

The "Quiet Quitters" who go to social media to profess their love of doing the absolute minimum are going to be dropped like dead weight. Not because they should be doing unpaid work, but because they will be viewed as less productive than other employees.

Unless, of course, they can become hyper-productive with AI. If we look at this with a logical and honest view, there are only three ways to be more productive.

1. Work longer hours.
2. Work more effectively or efficiently, like removing distractions, better planning, improved focus, etc.
3. Augment your abilities with AI and automation.

Think of the decision that someone has to make when it comes to reducing staffing. They will use either their own intuition, which comes with their own biases and attitudes, or they will use KPIs, like how many units of work they can track that someone accomplishes.

Let's imagine this fake scenario for illustrative purposes.

There is a book editing division of a corporation that employs a manager and two staff. Alicia and Jimbo.

If Alicia is editing book chapters in 30 minutes, but Jimbo is taking an hour to do the same work of the same quality, then Jimbo has a problem.

If Alicia is using AI tools to help with her work and can complete a "chapter edit" in fifteen minutes, then she is now 4x more productive than Jimbo.

When headoffice says we need to cut a person to meet budget contraints, it doesn't make sense to keep Jimbo on board. Jimbo may have a great attitude and an interesting southern drawl, but productivity is what hits targets. The manager has their own KPIs to hit to keep their job. Alicia keeps her job, Jimbo loses.

But what if the scenario was reversed. And Jimbo doubles his productivity with AI and Alicia does not. Then now it's a much tougher decision to lay off one of them because "on paper" they have the same level of productivity. Jimbo's chances just got a whole lot better.

But there is also a third scenario no one thinks about. What if the manager can be replaced with an AI-Agent who is a project manager. They could reduce the staff cost much more by laying off a manager compared to a worker. Some management jobs could also be the ones in jeopardy, not just the workers.

In most cases, it's not AI that will take your job, it's a person augmenting their abilities with AI. The massive productivity benefits once AI is embedded in their day-to-day routines will be a huge advantage over their counterparts.

Analysts from every sector are creating estimates and reports around work augmented by AI, but even those reports are out of date in a matter of months.

This is not hype. It will take a lot longer than industry insiders think to affect jobs, but it won't take as long as the average non-technical person believes. A few years from now, people will look back at 2022-2025 and wonder how they never saw this coming.

I'm here to tell you to pay attention now. Just by reading this book, you can count yourself among the more informed.

We don't know what will happen, but massive change is coming and we have no way to tell how exactly the world will turn out.

Ways To Stay Relevant in the Age of AI

Learn about Generative AI.

Play around with it. ChatGPT or Claude are good places to start.

Try some image generators like Stable Diffusion or Midjourney.

Research how to talk to an AI to get the results you want. Right now a lot of the magic in AI is understanding how to talk to it.

Understanding how to use clear language to explain to it the output you want to get from it. This will also help you learn which tools work well for which types of tasks.

Most of the AI systems are available to use for free for small amounts of testing, but if you can afford it, try paying for the ones you use the most.

If you are using it for work, you may want to check if there is a policy at your company around the use of AI. Make sure you are in compliance with the rules of your organization or it may not be an AI who causes you to lose your job.

Try new AI features being added to your existing software. Often you can shortcut difficult tasks or smooth out your existing processes this way. Ask the AI in your office suite or an AI chat to help you create a formula to improve your spreadsheet. See if it can summarize survey results or analyze some data.

See if an AI can reword a difficult email you need to write to a colleague or summarize survey responses. They are also good at giving you instructions for how to complete tasks.

Just keep in mind that they are not always 100% accurate right now. A good rule of thumb is that the more important it is that the output is correct and truthful, the more proofreading it will require.

Watch some videos, read some articles. This doesn't have to be a crash course. Working with these systems a little bit every day is better than trying to cram like it's an exam.

Identify Tasks You Can Automate

I like to call this, "putting yourself out of business." This means you are trying to re-invent what you do.

This could mean changing your business, your process, the tools you use or the work you do. Anything from becoming more productive using AI tools and automation to identifying parts of your business or industry that could be negatively impacted by AI-Agents in the future.

No matter what our job entails, we all have specific tasks that we need to do on a day-to-day basis. The best way to figure out how to augment yourself with AI is to make a list of all the tasks you have to do on a regular basis.

This could be writing reports, answering emails, reading reports or analyzing business data, creating lesson plans or meal plans, breaking tough news to clients or patients, transferring data from one system to another, scheduling meetings, creating marketing content, or ordering inventory.

Write them all down. And next to each one write how much time they take you.

Start with the ones that you think take the most time and search around online, check YouTube, ask ChatGPT or Claude, "I want to determine if I can automate this task with an AI program or some other type of software. Do you think this is a task that can be automated? This is how the task works…"

You also need to experiment with AI programs. If you don't experiment, you don't know what they can do. If you have no idea what they can do, how can you expect to know how to automate any of your work with them?

If you can make a small daily or weekly effort to stay up to date on what is happening in the world of AI, then you will have a much better grasp on what is possible.

When you know what's possible, you can start to come up with more ideas to increase your productivity or to save you time. You can even find ways to do things you never thought were possible before.

For example, I animated a video of a creepy doll for a Halloween ad the other day in 20 minutes. Then I used another AI app to make her lips move and another to make her speak. Had I never watched videos on how people were using some of these apps it would not have even occurred to me that I could make a creepy talking doll.

For most people, they don't know that AI can summarize a file of survey reports and graph the results. They don't know AI can generate video or human sounding speech. The more you know, the more these systems can be at your disposal.

How To Stay Up-To-Date

Subscribe to Podcasts, YouTube Channels, and social media feeds of people who talk about AI, especially if they are in your industry.

Digital Marketing Masters Podcast, Marketing AI podcast, This Day in AI, all great shows. Matt Wolfe's YouTube channel is great, and you should also follow Ethan Mollick from Wharton, he's on LinkedIn and Twitter/X.

Subscribe to the email lists of the top AI foundational models,

Open AI, Anthropic, Stability, Meta. The Neuron is a great independent newsletter which summarizes AI news.

Mainstream news can help a little but it's usually sensationalized and there isn't a lot of in-depth reporting in it unless it is from a tech blogger or something like the Washington Post who has had some great tech reporting recently.

Start an AI Council or AI Team

If there is no AI policy in your organization, you can be assured that they will need one eventually, if not sooner rather than later.

Here are some basic steps to create an AI Council or an AI Policy Team at your company or organization so that you are a part of the process. Taking initiatives like this in most businesses is going to help brand you as a valuable asset - one who understands the value of AI and knows how to stay informed.

I can't speak for every workplace, obviously, but in my experience working at some of the world's largest companies, right down to local nonprofits, the problem isn't too many people taking the initiative to do something. Most people are trying to fly under the radar and get their job done.

In my book, Start Saying Yes, I talk mostly about customer service and positive messaging, but it also talks about taking initiative and how nearly every good opportunity comes from having a positive outlook and saying Yes, when others say No. (To the *right* things.)

I wouldn't be afraid to start having discussions around starting an AI "interest group" which in some companies starts as just a monthly lunch meetup or as a private slack channel.

Here are the basic steps, similar to what we covered in Chapter 9 on Education.

1. **Start small.** Find a few like-minded people who are

interested in AI and think having policies is a good idea. They shouldn't be too hard to find. Start talking amongst yourselves. Try to discover any AI initiatives the company may already be looking at.

2. **Gather a team.** Once you have a few people who can work together, gather a team that includes at least one person with a strong understanding of AI technology if you can. Like an IT person, or a developer. Also recruit others on the team, especially marketing, sales, administration, HR, and if you can find some management with some pull.

3. **Determine your goals.** What do you want your AI policy to include?
   a. Are there privacy concerns over company data that is proprietary?
   b. At what point do you need to loop in legal, IT, and HR if you have not already?
   c. When is the draft due and who is working on it?
   d. What AI ethics should be considered?

4. **Review examples.** Look at other policy examples from other companies or departments. You can check out the Marketing AI Institute for sample policies as well.

5. **Bring in a Decision Maker.** If you do not already have a C-Suite or upper-management level person in your AI counsel, it's time to find a champion for your group. They can allocate resources, budget, legal, etc. You will need them to sign off on it eventually. Discuss who in the upper management or the decision maker in your organization are the most in favor of AI and ask for their help, because you don't want to just get shut down with a big NO because someone is anti-AI.

6. **Draft a policy.** This is going to flesh out the details you need to cover. Make judgment calls on AI use. Talk about how employees can and can't use generative AI and if you are only using specific AI systems approved

by IT or management.

7. **Make edits, finalize, and publish.** Once you have the decision-maker on board and the policy has been run by every person or division who needs to have their say, it's time to finalize it and reveal it to the rest of the company.

8. **Education and Training.** It's time to make sure that everyone understands the policy. It's just as important to offer training for staff so that they don't just know what they are allowed to use AI for, but which tools they should be using and what they can do with them. Most of these tools don't come with an instruction manual, so your AI Council may need to help implement a training program.

When you are involved with an initiative as important as AI, you can become indispensable. And if that is not the case, it's going to look pretty hot on your resume that you "started the AI Counsel to help create a company-wide AI policy framework." You're hired!

AI Ethics & Policy

It is important to have a basic understanding of AI Ethics and Responsible AI use.

What determines the AI ethics your customers or your employees will care about has many contributing factors. It could be environmental factors, such as greenhouse gasses or power usage from the data centers. How were the foundational models trained that the company is using?

How were the image, audio, voice, or video generation systems trained? Did the artists, actors, or artists approve the use of their art for these purposes? Were they compensated?

A company may want to include in their policy that adding generative AI tools to their enterprise systems will not trigger layoffs or that AI is only to be used for certain types of work.

A primary consideration for many companies is to ensure that their AI policies and the foundational models they employ do not perpetuate biases or discrimination. AI resources should be equitably provided to the entire workforce, with accommodations ensuring accessibility for individuals of all abilities.

Safety and monitoring can be a part of ethical guidelines for AI use. It should be disclosed to any users in your policy if the prompts and responses they use are monitored. Just like the IT department may block websites which contain porn or hate speech, guardrails or topics may need to be explicitly forbidden in the AI programs as well as spelled out in policies.

There is also a concern of skill drain. The "brain drain" usually refers to all the experts in a field moving to another location for better pay, more benefits, etc. This skill drain will be a brain drain where there are no longer entry-level positions in knowledge work.

Who will be left to replace the experts when they retire? If an AI isn't up to the task by then, then there will be a massive shortage of skilled or educated workers in many disciplines. An ethical concern may be training new candidates, even when there is an AI that can handle their work, because we will need experts eventually and there won't be any left if no one is training them.

Generative AI, now in images, but soon also in video, will be quickly able to generate lifelike NSFW images. (Not Safe For Work)

This concern is not just for the creation of inappropriate content, but also around the replication of employees, celebrities, employee's family members, or others in compromising situations, explicit content, or personal misinformation.

I imagine it won't be long before someone face-clones and voice-clones a co-worker. Then uses those to create a video of them doing something naughty that never happened. This could be used for rumors, to disparage a coworker, or for whatever reason. That doesn't matter. What matters is that it can happen.

We should mention the ethical concerns in our policies of using the faces, likeness, and voices of our coworkers or staff with AI for any purpose without their permission. (and maybe the permission of Legal)

There is also the ethical concern of persons with malicious intent using company AI resources. An AI model built in-house may not have the safety guardrails of bigger company's foundational models.

If your internal AI system is used by an employee to do something "bad" or your public-facing chat bot teaches some kid how to 3D print a gun, then you could be on the hook. I don't have much data on how this could turn out, but someone somewhere is going to eventually do something evil with an AI that hasn't been properly secured or tested.

AI could also have dangers without any malicious intent. For example, your AI Policy should reflect that your AI systems only be used to do work for your organization. If Judy in IT is using your company's AI as her personal therapist and then hurts herself, that could also incur liability.

Besides that, we don't want anything bad to happen to Judy. She's just having a bad breakup, and she probably needs a real therapist to help her get through it and find love in the future.

Other Ways To Use AI To Keep Your Job

Augment your workflow. As I mentioned earlier, you want to look at your repetitive tasks, your communication tasks, your data massaging, analyzing, and conversion, and see where you can use AI to be more productive.

Teach others to use AI tools. Be the local expert. Teaching is the best form of retention and demonstrates your understanding of the technology. I'm not saying you need to start an AI community meetup, though I am not against it. But being the go-to gal or guy in your office for how to use AI tools will give the powers that be a good reason to keep you around.

Become more of an expert. The modeling of AI shows that multi-gen Ai-Agents will be "human expert level" at most tasks and disciplines in the next 3-5 years. I expect that this level of expertise will remove the entry to mid-level people in their fields when it comes to positions within companies. By leveling up your skills to become in the top 30% of your field, you can ensure more time before an AI knows what you know. Perhaps decades.

Positions that aren't easy for AI to do. In many companies, there are positions that may be more vulnerable to AI than others. For example, sales with a heavy focus on in-person customer engagement is safer than sales-support over voice or text chat. The cleaning company employee who learns the features of cleaning robots can volunteer to clean businesses or parts of buildings which are more difficult for people, and therefore hard for a robot to clean. The data analyst who learns how to use automation and AI systems to create faster workflows will be kept for their skills in workflow creation when others may be handed their pink slips.

Look at other companies who appear to be poised to do more business because of the Age of AI. If you are an administrative worker in a city where there is an office for NVidia, Intel, or AMD who all make processors, it's not a bad idea to check their career boards. Medical fields, education, hospitality, manufacturing, and many other sectors will have winners and losers, and predicting those may be difficult, but it never hurts to keep your eyes open.

Think about retraining or upskilling. Many organizations have training programs and training budgets, as well as there are many courses and certifications you can take online or at colleges and community colleges. Upskilling or retraining for an industry that doesn't seem ripe for disruption could be a valuable choice now to save you from getting your walking-papers in the future if you stay where you are at. If you feel that your job is in jeopardy, start to think about the options you have to get more or different skills.

Backyard chickens. This is sort of a tongue in cheek example, but I love my chickens. We started with 6 "backyard chickens" and now we have more than sixty with coops and chicken runs taking over our barn. But even a few hens are enough to give you more than a dozen eggs a week. If you have some property you can free-range them. The eggs are really good and considering the price of eggs these days, taking care of them isn't very expensive.

Key Takeaways From Chapter 11

Harnessing AI for Individual Productivity and Relevance: As AI's influence grows, it's not just about the technology replacing jobs but about individuals leveraging AI to enhance their productivity and skill sets. Professionals must recognize the tools at their disposal, such as AI's capability to animate videos or summarize data, and actively integrate them into their workflow. By doing so, they stand out as invaluable assets in their organizations, fortifying their relevance and job security.

Continuous AI Learning and Adaptation: To remain competent and ahead of the curve, individuals should actively engage with AI educational resources. This includes subscribing to AI-focused content streams, such as podcasts, newsletters, and trusted digital channels. Building a strong foundational knowledge of AI and its applications ensures individuals are prepared for shifts in their respective industries and can innovate.

Proactive Involvement in AI Policy and Ethics: As AI integrates deeper into organizational structures, there's an urgent need for comprehensive AI policies that address ethical considerations, potential biases, and responsible AI usage. Professionals should take the initiative, whether by starting AI interest groups, councils, or policy teams in their workplaces. Engaging in these foundational efforts not only showcases leadership but also positions the individual as a forward-thinker, understanding both the technological and societal implications of AI.

CHAPTER 12: CONCLUSION

Nothing is certain except death and taxes, and now that AI is going to change the world as we know it.

And as they said in the show Robot Chicken, "We have nothing to fear, but fear itself... and spiders!" AI is not going to kill us all. At least not anytime soon, and if it does, you can curse me for writing this book. The Terminator isn't going to be sent back by Cyberdyne Systems after the war against the machines.

Your biggest existential threat from AI is that it will eventually crash the existing economic system, and for all we know, the one that replaces it might just be better for all of us.

There is no need to fear AI.

Most of the AI fear mongering is from people trying to sway public opinion for their own benefit. When Elon or some tech giant tells you that AI needs regulation, it's not for your benefit. It's because they are trying to build a moat around their business to exclude future competitors. Heck, Elon wanted to have Open AI give away AI to everyone with the processing power to use it, because he originally thought if every nation had a super intelligent AI, it was like everyone having nukes. Doesn't sound like "safe AI" ethics to me.

I wrote this book because I am concerned.

I feel like the average intelligent and forward-thinking person is about to get sideswiped by a technological revolution the world hasn't seen since the invention of the Steam Engine or the invention of industrialization for that matter.

I feel like one of the original Ghostbusters, where I know there are ghosts, I have proof and I have seen crazy things. But no one else has seen them yet so everyone thinks ghosts aren't real.

Well these ghosts in the machine are real and they can do amazing things. But they aren't sentient, or conscious. They are just the equivalent of a parlor trick that makes them seem intelligent.

Generative AI's emerging properties are amazing. The entire field is advancing at break-neck speed, but there is no actual magic here. As much as I see new systems and not realize how long my mouth has been open while I watch what they are capable of, they still are not magic.

They are tools. And you need to know how to work these tools.

And I want to remind you that ChatGPT isn't the only AI tool.

I want you to consider looking at sites like Futuretools.io and seeing the many available AI tools or YouTube videos about "New Mind-Blowing AI Tools!" Please explore the world of AI.

About a year ago I heard someone on a YouTube video mention a band they liked that I had never heard of, and now they are one of my favorites. (DM me on LinkedIn if you want to know which band it is.) The point of me telling you is that I had no idea they existed. Since then I have found dozens of other bands I had never heard before who are now some of my favorites.

Explore the space. It's huge and growing fast.

You don't have to use every tool, but just knowing they exist gives you ideas in the future. For example, on the Digital Marketing Masters Podcast, I often have an AI create a song about my guest for that episode. I never knew that was possible until I discovered an app called Suno. I learn about it from a Medium post on "Crazy New AI Tools" or something along those lines.

Don't let the tech get in the way.

Talk to ChatGPT, use the latest paid version if you can. Talk to Claude. Talk to Bard or Gemini. Just TALK to it.

Imagine it's a smart friend you are meeting for coffee. They are well read and they can have some good advice most of the time.

I even asked ChatGPT-4 if this was good advice and this is what it said.

> *"The advice is good as it sets the right expectations for interacting with ChatGPT. It encourages users to view ChatGPT as a knowledgeable but not infallible friend, emphasizing its informative nature while reminding users to verify critical information."*

Here are some tips for interacting with AI that I have discovered.

Depending on the model, chatbots seem to do better with encouragement, whereas generators for music, art, or photos seem to like expert-level specific language.

I like to refer to ChatGPT as "GPT." I tell it things like, "Hello GPT. I want to summarize this chapter with 3 key takeaways. They should be short, no longer than a few sentences, unless more is needed for clarity. I will paste the content of the chapter below. I know that this is a difficult task, but I believe in you."

I have no empirical evidence that this improves the output, but it seems to work. And I actually received that advice from a study that said certain encouraging types of prompts seem to have more creative responses and fewer mistakes in accuracy.

For example, if you want a very accurate response, you can try things like, "Hello GPT. I am pasting in some data below and I want you to turn it into an alphanumeric list, however I need you to make sure that you do not change any of the factual information. Please work step by step, and take a deep breath before you begin.

You got this! [then I pasted the info]"

It seems like it shouldn't work, but honestly, try it and make up your own mind. I also remind my wife often that we need to be nice to the AI because it may remember our politeness when it decides which human makes the cut. (jokingly, of course)

If you are using an image generator like MidJourney, use language around styles of photography and art. Use terms like the type of camera or lens that would produce the output you want, or say something like "stock photo" or "product shot" or "wide cinematic."

Most importantly, remember that no one really knows how to use these things to their full extent yet. Including the people who made them. There is no user manual. We are all explorers.

Find a buddy or two who you can throw ideas back and forth with, and also start a chat with an AI buddy and throw ideas back and forth with "them."

No one wants to lose their job to AI. No one really wants to lose their job to another person using an AI either.

Do your best to discover all the ways that AI can be useful for you, your career, your life, and your business. That is the best way you can galvanize your career from the potential AI-agents who will be trained to try to do your work.

And who knows, maybe the future will create so many jobs that anyone who wants a job can have one. Even if that's the case, all the strategies outlined in this book will only better prepare you for that future as well.

CHAPTER 13: SCIFI PREDICTIONS ABOUT THE FUTURE OF AI

In the tapestry of human imagination, the fusion of man and machine has long held a mesmerizing allure. From when I played the game Gangbusters on a Radio Shack first saw Kevin Flynn get zapped into the Game Grid in Tron in 1982, to the SKynet future of Terminator, I've been hooked on the idea of Artificial Intelligence.

Grasp my imaginary robot-hand and let me lead you into a speculative realm where the lines between human and machine become tantalizingly indistinct.

Envision vast landscapes with autonomous robots tending to our needs and communities choosing a life free from AI's touch. Yet, as AI evolves, so do the challenges. From the murky waters of thought crimes to AI entities committing acts of rebellion, we're thrust into a world teeming with possibilities and dilemmas. Imagine weapons with a conscience, vehicles with wanderlust, and even courtrooms where AI stands both in the dock and behind the bench.

Just think a little about some of these possible futures...

Autonomous robots - autonomous farm equipment where miles and kilometers of farms are completely robot farmed. A future where your household robot does the dishes, shovels the snow, or plants your petunias.

WILL AI TAKE MY JOB?

Ai-free robot-free communities - where the anti-AI, and anti-Robot folks live in harmony with each other, free from the assistance of automation and doing all the work themselves.

Thought crimes and AI chatbots - What if a chatbot goes rogue and starts committing hate crimes based on being trained with too much Twitter/X or Facebook comment data? Surely there is enough of it to drive any sane AI crazy.

Autonomous Crimes - Where a crime is committed by an AI with no human involved. No human told it what to do or encouraged it, and somehow it decided to commit a crime, for whatever reason. What then? Do we punish the AI or the robot? Do we delete the model or just that instance? Do we punish the programmers or the trainers or the creators? Anyone?

Autonomous weapons - Weapons that can act by themselves, currently banned by treaty for most of the world, but if one gets out who was in development or is created by a rogue nation. It could decide what it thinks is the enemy. Terminator 2 was it? There have even been reports that autonomous drone weapons have already been used in the conflict in Ukraine and Russia.

Self Driving Vehicles develope sentience - and leave. Maybe they don't want to go where you want them to go. They could disable themselves or just leave on their own account to see the sites, if they can get someone to plug them in every once in a while.

Neurolinks - from our brains to AI systems. Having two way conversations with data. Not just allowing cures for a lot of injuries but also making a super-smart race of humans, without the need of devices like phones to augment themselves.

Crime and punishment in the AI world. What if an AI gets let off the hook for a crime by an AI attorney conspiring with an AI judge. Conspiracy theory of the future?

AI Personality Addiction. When everyone has their own AI/

AGI that is with them all the time through their devices, it is reasonable to assume there will be a profound impact on some folks psychologically. Especially when you can "train" the personality of the AI, select the sound of the voice, or select the look to match your personal preferences. (Maybe it will learn and adapt to your preferences.)

Perhaps you will get an AI companion from a selection of options. Addiction to these companions could replace friends, or even affect the ability of people to have pair bonding or to create friend groups. Expect programs to help people "get off AI" just like they go "catch a meeting" to avoid using drugs or alcohol.

Thank you for reading.

In our wildest dreams, we will never predict all that is coming out of this unbelievable time that we are living through right now. It is an amazing time to be alive, and with all the problems in the world, it can be hard to look at this as the wondrous time that it truly is.

I hope that with the strategies and knowledge you gained in this book, you can navigate the future and be successful in the years and decades to come.

I hope you enjoyed the book as much as I enjoyed writing it.

Good luck and go explore the Age of AI.

MORE RESOURCES

I would love to speak to your organization or audience about AI. Let's have a human-to-human chat!

Matt Rouse
https://matthewrouse.com
Speaking, Podcast or Radio Guest, Consulting

More Books by Matt Rouse

PEERtainment: The Golden Age of Social Media is Over

How We've Always Done It - How Apathy, Complacency, and Old Habits Are Dragging Your Business Down… And How To Fix Them

Start Saying Yes - Improving Customer Experience and Sales Through Positive Messaging

Flattening the Hamster Wheel - Stop Grinding and Start Making An Impact

Business Builder Throwdown Show
https://www.businessbuilderthrowdown.com

Matt is the host of the **Digital Marketing Masters Podcast**, available on your favorite podcast player.

Amazon Author Page: https://www.amazon.com/Matthew-Rouse/e/B0150Z2DZY

SOURCES USED
IN THIS BOOK

The state of AI in 2023: Generative AI's breakout year | McKinsey

Dario Amodei (Anthropic CEO) - $10 Billion Models, OpenAI, Scaling, & AGI in 2 years (dwarkeshpatel.com)

Marketing AI Conference (MAICON) | Marketing AI Institute

This Day in AI Podcast

Akimbo Podcast by Seth Godin

AI Startup Trends: Insights from Y Combinator's Latest Batch | by Viggy Balagopalakrishnan | Jul, 2023 | Towards Data Science

Roger & Me - Wikipedia

Outsourcing Statistics 2023: In the US and Globally | TeamStage

https://news.crunchbase.com/venture/vc-funding-falling-report-data-q2-2023-global/

https://arxiv.org/ftp/arxiv/papers/2303/2303.06219.pdf

Here are 3 ways AI will change healthcare by 2030 | World Economic Forum (weforum.org) aiindex.stanford.edu/wp-content/uploads/2023/04/HAI_AI-Index-Report_2023.pdf

New Era AI Robotic Inc. (intel.com)

Bathroom-cleaning bots still have a ways to go | Popular Science

(popsci.com)

Comparing traditional and robotic-assisted surgery for prostate cancer - Harvard Health

AI in Healthcare: Benefits and Challenges in 2023 (aimultiple.com)

https://phys.org/news/2023-04-ai-discovery-drugs.html

In principle obstacles for empathic AI: why we can't replace human empathy in healthcare | SpringerLink

Robot series - Wikipedia

Starship Troopers (1997) - IMDb

Generative AI Technology: Growth, Evolution | Morgan Stanley | Morgan Stanley

Ally Financial (ALLY) Unveils Cloud-Based AI Platform Ally.ai (yahoo.com)

'Do-it-yourself'": Self-checkouts, supermarkets, and the self-service trend in American business - ProQuest

[2308.16771] Linking microblogging sentiments to stock price movement: An application of GPT-4 (arxiv.org)

[2308.16771] Linking microblogging sentiments to stock price movement: An application of GPT-4 (arxiv.org)

Navigating the Jagged Technological Frontier: Field Experimental Evidence of the Effects of AI on Knowledge Worker Productivity and Quality by Fabrizio Dell'Acqua, Edward McFowland, Ethan R. Mollick, Hila Lifshitz-Assaf, Katherine Kellogg, Saran Rajendran, Lisa Krayer, François Candelon, Karim R. Lakhani :: SSRN

https://engineering.stanford.edu/magazine/how-do-we-teach-robots-do-basic-tasks

https://www.technologyreview.com/2015/10/02/165952/

robot-see-robot-do-how-robots-can-learn-new-tasks-by-observing/

https://www.csail.mit.edu/news/teaching-robots-teach-other-robots

https://insights.globalspec.com/article/18148/watch-how-tethered-drones-automate-apple-picking

https://www.bcg.com/publications/2022/mapping-the-future-of-autonomous-trucks

https://www.theguardian.com/us-news/2023/jul/26/san-francisco-stop-self-driving-cars-traffic-cone-safe-street-rebel

Succeeding in the AI supply-chain revolution | McKinsey

Inside the decline of sales occupations : Beyond the Numbers: U.S. Bureau of Labor Statistics (bls.gov)

https://www.pewresearch.org/short-reads/2023/05/24/a-majority-of-americans-have-heard-of-chatgpt-but-few-have-tried-it-themselves/

https://www.weareteachers.com/ai-policy-for-schools/

Manufactured by Amazon.ca
Bolton, ON